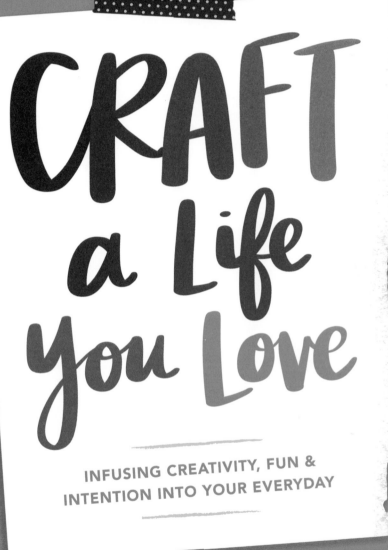

CRAFT a Life You Love

INFUSING CREATIVITY, FUN & INTENTION INTO YOUR EVERYDAY

AMY TANGERINE

Abrams Image, New York

Editor: Cristina Garces
Designer: Danielle Young
Production Manager: Rebecca Westall

Library of Congress Control Number: 2017944948

ISBN: 978-1-4197-3006-1

Printed and bound in China
10 9 8 7 6 5 4 3 2 1

Abrams books are available at special discounts when purchased in
quantity for premiums and promotions as well as fundraising or educational
use. Special editions can also be created to specification. For details,
contact specialsales@abramsbooks.com or the address below.

ABRAMS The Art of Books
195 Broadway, New York, NY 10007
abramsbooks.com

To JC and Jack:

The family we've created is everything.

Thanks for showing me a happiness
I never knew before, and for putting up
with all my crafts and crazy ideas.

You inspire me to be
a better person every day.

All my love.

CONTENTS

———

INTRODUCTION 8

PART ONE
Crafting the Soul

The Most Important Part of Your Day (It's Not Breakfast!) 12
The Mermaid Dress 20
You Are Weird and Quirky 24
You Are Weird and Quirky, Part II 28
Loving Yourself 36

PART TWO
Crafting the Right Mindset

Feeding the Good Wolf 46
Right Time, Right Place? Rubbish! 53
The Gift of Evidence 58
Be Grateful for Everything You Do Not Have 62
I Will Not Complain. I Will Not Complain. I Will Not Complain. 68

PART THREE
Crafting the Right Environment

You're Gonna Need a Bigger Boat 76
You Have Enough Time 83
The One Question 88
The Rule of Positivity 94
Willpower 100

PART FOUR
Crafting Happiness Through Habits

Turning Happiness into a Habit   106
Jack's Bedtime Ritual   114
When No One Else Is Awake   116
Looking Somewhere Else   120
Detox   126

PART FIVE
Crafting Your Way Back

On Losing Your Creative Mojo   132
Easy Does It   136
Thinking Inside the Box   140
Lost . . . in the Right Place   144
On Waiting It Out   150

PART SIX
Crafting Your Passions

No Doubt   158
Work Your Way Through It   160
Coming to the Crossroads   162
Focus, Dream, Live   164

WHAT'S NEXT?   170
ACKNOWLEDGMENTS   173
ABOUT THE AUTHOR   175

INTRODUCTION

—

This book will take you on a journey into the past and into the future. My main goal is to give you the tools for reflection so that you can craft a life that you love *today*. It has been broken into six sections, with each section representing a different stage of the process of crafting a life you love.

- In Part One, Crafting the Soul, we learn why crafting is so important and, specifically, how to discover what it is that you love to do. You will get permission to spend time crafting each and every day, and you will see that, in fact, spending time developing your hobbies might just be the most important part of your day.

- In Part Two, Crafting the Right Mindset, we examine how to reframe your thoughts and outlook to better position yourself to grab control of your own happiness.

- In Part Three, Crafting the Right Environment, we look at your environment—physical and mental—and discuss how to change and update your surroundings to live the best possible life.

- Part Four, Crafting Happiness Through Habits, is packed with some of my favorite practical tips for creating positive habits to feed your creative soul.

- Part Five, Crafting Your Way Back, and Part Six, Crafting Your Passions (a brand-new chapter created for this new edition of the book!), give you tools and inspiration for the future.

Each chapter of this book ends with an exercise (or practice) to help you move one step closer to the life of your dreams. I invite you to use colored pencils, to doodle, and to journal in every corner of this book.

Make it yours.

—AMY

PART ONE

—

crafting the SOUL

the most important part of your day (it's not breakfast!)

———

We hear a lot of clichés about believing in ourselves, about how we are perfect just the way we are, and how we cannot love anyone else until we learn how to love ourselves. From the time we are children, most of us are told to reach for the stars and dream big because we can be anything we want to be.

There is some truth to all those clichés, but each of them ignores a big part of the equation: You probably cannot feel good about yourself unless you are participating in things that you feel good doing.

This is one of the reasons I am such a huge proponent of taking time to cultivate your craft and to integrate your hobbies and side projects into your daily routine. Your hobbies might seem trivial to other people—I can assure you that plenty of people have let me know that they think scrapbooking is a silly and outdated hobby—but participating in your chosen hobby is an important part of feeling good, building confidence, and infusing happiness into your days.

This is why creation is not a luxury. It is a necessity.

You will probably have a hard time cultivating feelings of confidence and happiness simply by telling yourself that you should feel confident, believe in yourself, and love yourself just the way that you are. You need to engage in activities and behaviors that reinforce good feelings. Something magical happens when you prioritize your hobbies: You cultivate the feelings of being happy, believing in yourself, and loving yourself. You participate in and become aware of positive behaviors. You cannot help being happy and feeling confident when you are actively engaged in hobbies and side projects that bring you joy.

It seems so simple, doesn't it? Yet so many of our days are packed with things we *should* be doing, such as driving our kids to school, running errands, working, and making dinner. A lot of us spend the vast majority of our days serving other people, but, sadly, we fail to spend quality time serving ourselves. The side projects, crafts, and hobbies we want to do get pushed to the back burner day after day. No wonder people can go from loving their lives to feeling dissatisfied in tiny incremental steps, without even recognizing what went wrong.

Often, what went wrong is that you did not carve out five minutes here and ten minutes there to do things that make you feel good!

> **Don't ask yourself what the world needs. Ask yourself what makes you come alive, and go do that, because what the world needs is people who have come alive.**
> —HOWARD THURMAN

It does not matter if you love making tiny birds out of origami paper, baking elaborate cakes, or knitting baby socks. Your hobbies are important because they feed your soul. Never feel ashamed of them and never feel guilty for carving out time for them. In fact, your hobbies might be the most important part of your day. How can you be the best employee, the best partner, the best parent, or the best friend unless you feel your best?

My dad made his living as an engineer, but he also built furniture in his spare time. He did this in part to save money, but he was mainly driven by the desire to work with two-by-fours and to design and construct furniture from start to finish. He was also an amateur photographer and he played tennis at least twice a week. When I watched him participate in these activities, I could see the joy on his face. It was palpable.

I bet you know people who have hobbies that make them feel childlike and alive. My mom gets giddy when she sees my son, Jack, wearing something she hand-stitched. JC, Jack's dad and arguably my better half, is full of energy when he is in the kitchen cooking an entire meal for family and friends. I practically bounce around when the subject of crafting comes up.

What do you love doing?

When are you most inspired to do this?

Can you carve out at least ten minutes to do this each and every day? (Spoiler alert: The answer is yes!)

Here is your permission slip.

THIS IS YOUR

permission slip

DATE : 05 / 23 / 22

NAME : Lisa Fuller

The most important part of my day is the part where I take care of myself and feed my soul. I cannot be the best partner, the best employee, the best boss, the best parent, or the best friend if I am not at my best. Therefore, I have permission, each and every day, to pursue my craft in order to take loving care of myself and be my best self for the most important people in my life.

X _____

sign here

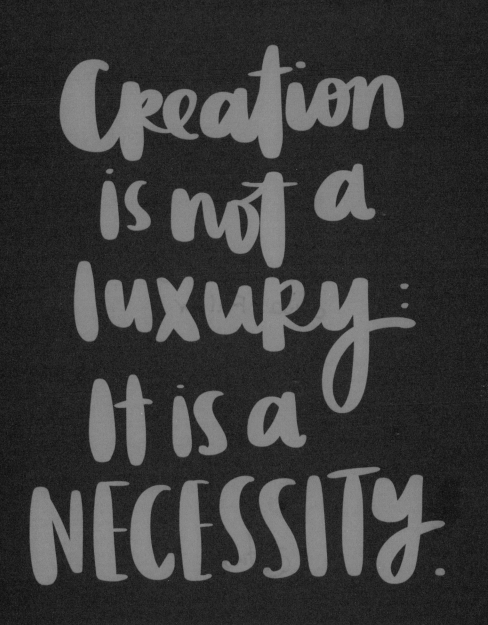

CRAFT A LIFE YOU LOVE

Tomorrow, keep track of your activities, such as
working, exercising, cooking, and running errands, and
notice how you feel. Rate your happiness on a scale
of 1 (drained) to 10 (awesome).

ACTIVITY	HOW I FEEL (1–10)	NOTES
Making the bed	10	I have already accomplished something right after getting up!
Running	8	I need to do this in the morning
Checking/ responding to email	3	Need to find a better system for this
Blogging	5	Love sharing, but posts take a lot of time
Editing videos	8	Takes a long time, but I enjoy the process

ACTIVITY	HOW I FEEL (1–10)	NOTES
Walking	10	I enjoy the morning walks
Making the bed.	8	It takes time
Exercising	9	I need to do this. Gained weight
Preparing my lunch	7	Takes time but I enjoy eating healthy.
Travelling to Work	5	Have to take a taxi. Need a car
Working in someone's house	4	Do not enjoy. Not my space. Grateful for the income, however
Spending time with friends	10	I enjoy the company

ACTIVITY	HOW I FEEL (1–10)	NOTES
Watching T.V.	8	I could be more productive
Getting up to pray	10	It builds my spiritual life
Texting my children	9	I wish they were close by. Miss them but happy to text them.

At the end of the day, review the list. If there are more draining activities in your day than awesome ones, consider how you can cultivate your hobbies and replace some of these draining activities with ones that make you happy. Of course there will be obligations and responsibilities that we cannot avoid. This is why it is important to identify the fulfilling ones and reframe our thoughts about the activities we do not enjoy as much.

the mermaid dress

My friend Laura asked me to make her prom dress when we were in high school. She imagined a sleeveless, bright aqua blue dress with a choker collar and a fit that hugged the waist and hips and flared at the knees like a mermaid's tail.

When she described what she wanted, I could picture the dress perfectly. (If you were a teenage girl in the 1990s, this was your dream dress.) And I knew I could make it.

Laura and I went shopping together about three weeks before the prom. We picked out the fabric and found two patterns from which we pieced together a custom dress, which included six panels and lining. Then I measured Laura and got to work.

A week before the prom, I took the dress to Laura for the fitting. I don't remember if she cried in front of me, but she did gasp—the dress was too small and would not zip up all the way. I had made a slight mistake (whoopsy!) in calculating the seams and, because the dress was paneled, the mistake was repeated multiple times, resulting in a dress that was too tight even for Laura's tiny frame.

There we stood, a week before what was to be the highlight of our lives to date, and I had made a terrible blunder.

Here is the kicker: I panicked only slightly, and I regained my composure quickly. Confidence kicked in. I knew how to sew, and I knew I could fix the mistake. I carefully took apart the dress and made the adjustments. To remove the needle holes that were showing in the fabric, I steamed the dress. It worked like magic. A week later, Laura wore that mermaid dress with pride. (And five years later, she married her prom date.)

I think about this story when I am reflecting on the changes that have occurred in my life. The truth is that, while I have thankfully grown and evolved quite a bit as a person since high school, the things that I love to do remain the same. I loved sewing then and I still do today. I have always felt confident and happy behind the sewing machine. I loved making big, colorful collages back then, and today, I love making scrapbooks. I loved reading inspirational quotes then; the same is still true today.

Hobbies can be our through-line in life, our stabilizing constant during transitions. Sometimes, we lose sight of who we are. We become parents, change jobs, or lose our romantic partners, and we feel lost. Our hobbies can keep us stable. They remind us that we are more than employees, more than spouses, more than parents, and more than friends. And our hobbies are more than diversions: They are woven into the fabric of our identity and they remind us that we know how to do things. When we are feeling low, we can jump on that horse, pick up that violin, or string that wrap bracelet and do something that feels good and lifts us up.

When we learn how to do something well—whether it is riding a horse or playing the violin or making jewelry—it feeds our confidence, which we can draw upon later. When we encounter obstacles, instead of feeling inept, we know that there is at least one thing we can do well. Knowing that I could fix Laura's prom dress might seem insignificant, but, during life's transitions, small confidence boosters like this can fuel your stamina and make you feel powerful. This is yet another reason I say that creation is not a luxury; it is a necessity.

I have changed colleges, moved across the country, been laid off, started businesses, become a mother, given up on certain aspects of my company, ended relationships, and started new relationships. Through it all, my hobbies have been constant, reminding me of who I am and that I am powerful and joyful. They have played a key role in perfecting the art of living honestly.

CRAFT A LIFE YOU LOVE

Sometimes, all of life's *shoulds* take us away from who we are and what we want to do. Looking back to earlier years, when life was simpler, can remind us of our passions. Ask yourself these questions:

What did I love to do when I was in elementary school, junior high, or high school?

I loved to play netball,
I love to read and cook.

How did I feel when I was doing what I loved?

I felt very happy and fulfilled

Would I still love doing that today?

Oh yes

What are some things I am good at?

Cooking, baking, helping other people, organising.

What do I love doing now, as an adult?

I love to watch the television
I love to worship, love to cook.
I Love helping people

Everyone's lives go through a series of transitions
like moves, job changes, and becoming parents.
What are some of your life's transitions?

Getting married, becoming a parent, job as a teacher & moving to another country

How did your hobbies help you during these times?

Being loving and caring, help me as a parent & teacher

List some of the titles you most identify with. Think
through the roles you are most proud of as if you were
being interviewed for a profile piece. For example,
I would put "I am a hard-working creator, a fun-loving
and supportive mama, who tries to be fearless in the
pursuit of what makes me happy."

I am a determined and caring mother who works very hard to support my kids. I am a fun-loving and strong teacher who wears many hats.

Look at all of the characteristics you listed, and make
a bold statement:

I love to

you are weird and quirky

—

I t is easy to get caught in the comparison trap. I know I do it. When I first started scrapbooking, I thought that I would never be as good as some of the other paper crafters out there, so pursuing scrapbooking as a career felt a little bit ridiculous.

Then my friend's seven-year-old son reminded me of something important. He was preparing for his swim meet, and he asked his mom, "Do you think I'll beat my personal best?"

"Probably," she said. "You have been working really hard."

The conversation made an impression on me because he didn't ask whether he would win or get a medal. He simply wondered whether he would do his best. No one else's time was important to him. It reminded me of a famous Mikhail Baryshnikov quote: "I do not try to dance better than anyone else. I only try to dance better than myself."

You will never be able to do things the same way that other people do them, so stop trying. It's a meaningless battle. Every person is a unique constellation of talents and abilities, so you can't share another person's benchmarks.

If this disappoints you, consider that the reverse is also true: It doesn't matter how many people do what you do. No one else can do it like you. You need to focus on your strengths and talents.

When you stop trying to mimic other people and instead decide to be you, something wonderful happens: A whole world of colors, fabrics, textures, words, emotions, sounds, and flavors present themselves to you.

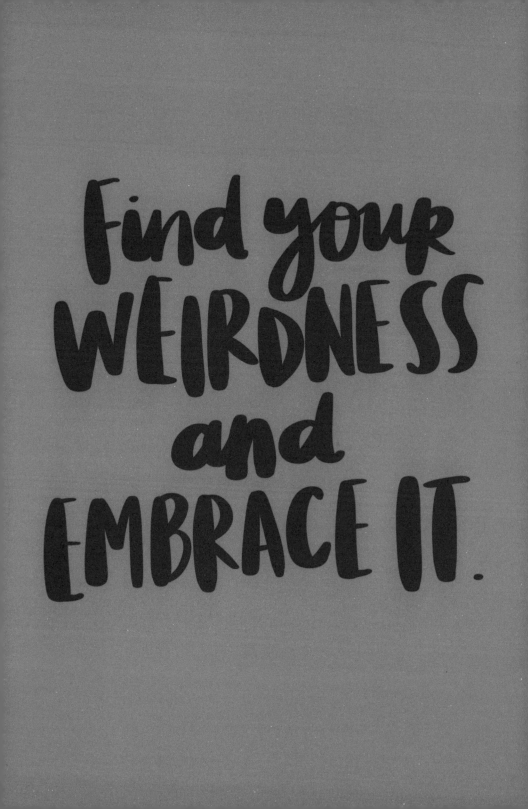

Unconstrained by what everyone else is doing, you become the creator of your own life.

Bradley Hart is an example of this: He paints portraits . . . sort of. Bradley injects paint into syringes and then fills each individual bubble in a sheet of bubble wrap with paint, as if the bubbles are pixels. Is he the best painter in the world? Would you even call him a painter? I don't know, but I do know that no one else in the world is Bradley Hart.

No one else is you. And no one else is me. So let's stop comparing ourselves to others.

Looking to other artists for inspiration is a great way to get motivated. If you enjoy trying to re-create another artist's work for personal use, by all means, go for it! I can assure you that I have spent more than a couple of hours on Pinterest getting ideas for different craft projects. But using other people as a standard for judging yourself is pointless. If you spend your life trying to imitate other people, you will not have time to discover what makes you unique.

"Imperfections are not inadequacies; they are reminders that we're all in this together."

—BRENÉ BROWN

Seeing your own uniqueness can be difficult, especially if you are caught in the trap of comparison. Because you live with yourself all day long, everything you do probably seems normal to you.

But I can assure you that you are not normal. You are weird and quirky—in a good way. You do things that no one else does. You have thoughts and dreams and abilities that, when packaged together, are highly unusual. The trick is to find your weirdness and embrace it.

CRAFT A LIFE YOU LOVE

So what makes you weird and quirky? Ask around. Ask the people who love you the most—your best friends, your partner, your siblings, and your parents—the following questions:

What do you like most about me?

Very Kind and God-fearing

What do I do that no one else does?

Extra caring towards others

How am I weird and crazy?

Just get upset at anytime. Laugh alot for everything.

Eventually, you will start to see yourself through the eyes of the people who love you the most. You will see that you are, indeed, a bizarre human being—and that this is what makes you special.

Then embrace yourself. Lean in. Feed the quirk. Even if your weirdness seems as if it has nothing to do with your hobbies or your craft, feeding your weirdness will inspire you. When you allow your unique self to rise to the surface, you will feel more stimulated and alive. You will understand that you are valued, treasured, and special in this world. Honoring this, and loving yourself for it, will fuel that little glimmer inside your soul that drives you to create, design, and live your life to its fullest.

you are weird and quirky, part II

—

I went to high school with a good-looking, kind, popular football player who was on the student council. I cannot remember for sure, but I suspect he was Homecoming King (or at least nominated). Let's call him Clint.

I got to know Clint better because he was in my sewing class.

That's right—good-looking, kind, popular, probably-Homecoming-King Clint signed up for sewing as an elective.

Doesn't this just make you smile? I know it makes me happy to think back on the delight and exuberance that filled his face when he finished making his first pair of boxer shorts. Clint certainly did not fit the profile of the kind of teenager who signed up for sewing as an elective, but he did it anyway. He did not care that the stereotypical football player did not sew. He liked what he liked, unapologetically.

At the time, I was going through a big transition. My dad and I had moved from Chicago to Atlanta the summer before high school started. My mom was scheduled to arrive the following year when she wrapped up her job. I was not consciously aware of it then, but this move marked the beginning stages of my parents' ultimate divorce.

So there I was, making the difficult transition from junior high to high school in a new part of the country without much of a support system nearby. I had moved seven hundred miles from the only place I knew as home. Most of my friends and family were still in Chicago and, while I was happy to be with my dad in Atlanta, I missed my mom and my grandparents.

Making matters worse, I felt ethnic tension for the first time in my life. When I walked through the doors of high school on that first day, I saw clusters of people who were obviously separated by ethnicity. When I lived in the northern suburbs of Chicago, I had friends of many different ethnicities and had never much considered it as either positive or negative. At my new high school, it definitely seemed like an issue.

More than two thousand students attended my high school, and only about ten of them were Asian. I wanted to find my people—to fit in somewhere—but I was neither black nor white, and I did not even relate to "being Asian." I eventually made friends, and some of them were Asian, but that was never the reason for our friendship. I was friends with people who had common interests and values.

I found myself reflecting on what it meant to be *me*. I was the new kid, already an outsider, struggling to fit in at a place where I thought people fit in based on their ethnicity, but I didn't feel like I belonged to any particular ethnic group, personality-wise. In retrospect, this was a big opportunity for me: I had to let my individuality shine through. I had to find my own unique way. Clint, the football-playing sewer, unwittingly gave me permission to be myself. I loved sewing and making collages and writing in fancy cursive. It made me feel happy and joyful, and if a football player could defy categories and be accepted for who he was, I could be accepted for who I was, too!

I am telling you this because you will always feel better if you are just *you* instead of worrying about the box you think you are supposed to fit in. All around you are people who are worried about what they are supposed to look like, act like, talk like, and be like. If you take a close look, you will see that they are not nearly as happy as the "weirdos" who follow their own path. The Clints of the world will stand out because they are practically glowing with confidence and happiness.

You do not have to live within anyone's paradigm. You can create your own. You are more than a spouse, a parent, a child, a sibling, a scrapbooker, or a crafter. You are so much more than a statistic or a tradition. You are unique, quirky, uncommon, and wonderful—just like Clint.

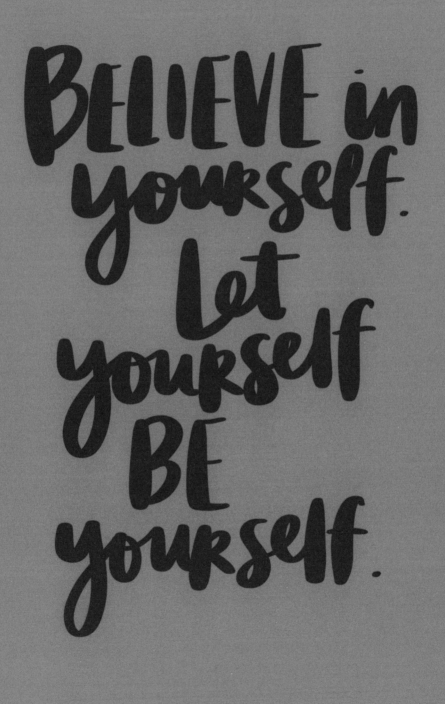

In the months after my son was born, I lost this perspective.

Being a mother felt all-consuming, and I believed that I had to be the perfect stereotypical mother, giving every ounce of energy to my son. I know that I am not the only new mother who has felt lost and confused in this new role. Each moment that we spend away from our children can feel shameful. When we walk out of our houses without our babies, when we try to squeeze in work emails or calls, and when we take showers while our infants coo in their cribs, we feel incredible guilt. Regaining a sense of balance can seem out of reach. Once I gave myself grace and accepted that I needed to focus on myself every once in a while, I was able to ultimately be a better mom.

Has something similar happened to you? If so, now is a good time to remind yourself that if you want to give your best to the people you love, you have to be you. You have to stop worrying about whether you are being "perfect" and start embracing all of the unique qualities that make you *you*.

I am not merely what I am labeled—not simply a mother or an Asian or a scrapbooker. None of us fits neatly inside any box. We are all bigger than that. We spill out of the boundaries, we color outside the lines, and we craft our own lives—and we can do so joyfully and without apology.

CRAFT A LIFE YOU LOVE

First, a quick story: When I was a young child, my parents both worked, so I spent a lot of time with my grandparents. When I was almost five, my parents enrolled me in kindergarten. There was one problem: I didn't speak English. Though my parents both spoke English and two dialects of Chinese—Hakka and Mandarin—all of the adults in my life, my grandparents included, spoke only Chinese in my presence. My parents were a bit worried; they wanted me to speak and understand English, of course, but they were concerned about the transition. How would I feel in a new environment filled with strangers who spoke a language they thought I did not understand?

Here is what my parents did not consider: I spent *a lot* of time watching *Sesame Street* while in the care of my grandparents. The amount of screen time I was allowed as a youngster would shock today's parents, but back then, it seemed acceptable for my grandparents to plop me in front of the TV and let the Muppets entertain me.

There was a certain wisdom in my grandparents' approach: From Big Bird, Bert, Ernie, and Oscar the Grouch, I learned English. No one told me that the characters on *Sesame Street* were speaking English, so I was not aware that I was learning until I walked through the doors of my kindergarten classroom.

My teacher welcomed me and directed me to my locker—and guess what?

I understood her! I stood there, beaming inside, as I connected the dots: This was the language that all the characters spoke on *Sesame Street*. It was English, and I understood it. I had learned it all on my own. I knew something that my parents and my grandparents did not teach me.

I was filled with pride as I realized what it meant to be *me.* I was someone separate and distinct from everyone else. I could learn things, do things, and create things that were simply . . . me. I was unique. I had a mind and a heart and could do things on my own.

So who are you? What does it mean to be *you?* Do you even know yet?

Since we are on the topic of *Sesame Street,* make an ABC list. This is a simple practice using the letters of the alphabet as prompts to write down twenty-six things that are inspiring to you or that define you. Jot down the things that make you uniquely *you,* or feel free to mix it up with a few things that you want to invite into your life.

A wesome

B rave

C aring

D ynamic | delightful

E ducated | Elegant

F aithful | friendly

G rateful | Gifted

H elpful

I ntelligent

J ovial

K ind

L oving

M usical

N ice

O bservant

P leasant

Q uiet / quirky

R eserved / Relatable

S trong

T houghtful

U nique

V ery caring

W eird (I filled in this one for you because you are weird.)

X

Y outhful

Z ealous

the ABC's of me

name _Lisa Fuller_

date _25 / 5 / 22_

loving yourself

❝I saw that you were perfect, and so I loved you. Then I saw that you were not perfect, and I loved you even more.❞

—ANGELITA LIM

I bet it's easy for you to read this quote and think about your children or your spouse. I know that I loved my son, Jack, from the moment I saw him, and I have loved him more every day since. He has grown from my perfect baby to a toddler who is filled with personality and quirks and, yes, even flaws. My most important job as his mother is to love him unconditionally, knowing that his flaws are what make him vulnerable and real.

It's also easy for me to read these words and think about my partner, JC, knowing that it is an honor to bear witness to his life, which includes not only his successes but also his missteps. It is a privilege and a pleasure to see him grow and evolve as we navigate this life together.

You can probably think of a few people in your own life whom you love, even more so because they are imperfect.

Do you apply the same love, compassion, and warmth to yourself?

It is hard to be your best creative self when you do not practice self-acceptance and forgiveness, so before we move forward to the next section, let us take a minute (or longer) to remember why this is so important.

When you run yourself down instead of build yourself up, you will have a hard time living your best life. Remember, you are unable to give your best if you do not feel your best. You cannot be the best parent, the best partner, the best friend, or the best whatever if you feel lousy.

So how do you let go of your shame and guilt? How do you forgive yourself?

Here is a trick that I use when I let myself down. I ask, "If the person I love most in the world did this, would I forgive him or her?"

The answer is always *yes*.

It's easy to forgive the people you love, and to love them even more because of their weaknesses. Why don't we do the same for ourselves?

Imagine that your young child stole a candy bar from the store. Instead of forgiving him, you tell him over and over again that he is a thief. When he lies, you tell him that he is a thief and a liar. When he is caught cheating on a test, you add "cheater" to the list of infractions. Imagine what kind of person your child would become if he constantly heard how awful he is!

You probably would never do this to your child. If you are like most parents, you forgive misdeeds, and you recognize that mistakes are opportunities for you to step in and teach lessons. You approach these situations with an understanding heart. You probably use kind words, knowing the power of your language molds and shapes character and self-esteem.

The same is true of your own character and self-esteem! Stop berating yourself for every misstep. When you make a mistake, use the opportunity to take a quiet breath and ask yourself what lesson you can take from it, so that you can grow from the experience. The list of potential transgressions that you could have made is long, and this is a good thing. Every mistake that you make represents an opportunity for you to learn, grow, and become a better version of yourself. Allow yourself to let go of shame and guilt and bad feelings. Give yourself grace.

66 **Many times what we perceive as an error or failure is actually a gift. And eventually we find that lessons learned from that discouraging experience prove to be of great worth.** 99

—RICHELLE E. GOODRICH

CRAFT A LIFE YOU LOVE

As you take part in your craft or hobby, reflect on these questions:

What is a "mistake" I have made?

_____

_____

_____

_____

_____

Did I learn something from this mistake or did it end up serving me in some way? (Perhaps you lost a job, which ended up being a good thing because you discovered your passion or found a better job as a result.)

_____

_____

_____

_____

_____

_____

_____

_____

_____

Would I forgive a loved one if he or she made this mistake?

_____

_____

_____

_____

What guilt or shame am I carrying around?

_____

_____

_____

_____

_____

_____

_____

_____

Then, before moving to Part Two, take fifteen minutes to journal on the following pages, reflecting on how your mistakes can turn you into a better person. Write down your thoughts and end your journal entry with these words: "I forgive myself."

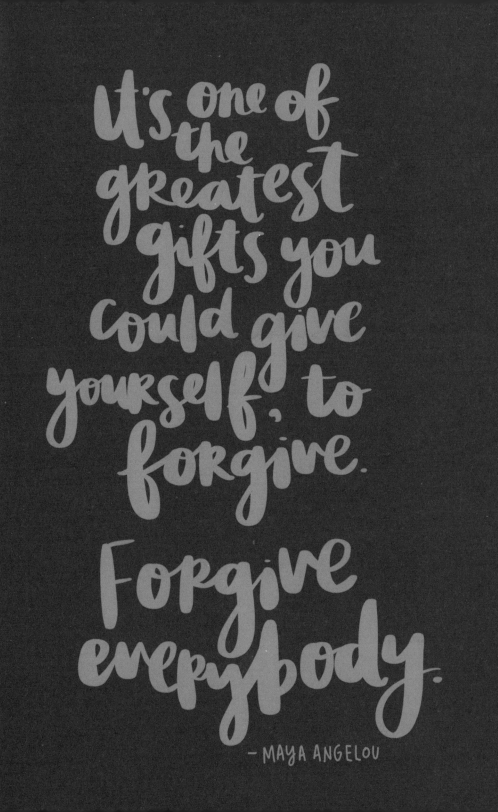

It's one of the greatest gifts you could give yourself, to forgive. Forgive everybody.

—MAYA ANGELOU

PART TWO

—

crafting the
RIGHT MINDSET

feeding the good wolf

———

A dear friend recently shared an old Cherokee legend with me called "The Two Wolves." In the legend, a grandfather tells his grandson about a fight going on inside all of us as if it were between two wolves. One wolf is evil: He is anger, envy, resentment, inferiority, and lies. The other is good: He is joy, peace, love, hope, serenity, humility, goodness, and truth.

The grandson thinks about this for a minute and then asks, "Which wolf will win?"

The grandfather's reply comes quickly: "The one you feed."

I love this story because it reminds me that **you are the creator of your own happiness.**

If you want to live your best life, it is clear which wolf you should feed. Feed the wolf that believes you are amazing, inspiring, and creative. That wolf needs to be stronger than the wolf that believes you are lazy, jealous, and dull. Self-confidence needs to be stronger than self-doubt; motivation needs to be more powerful than discouragement; and love needs to be more powerful than apathy.

But often, if you are not paying attention, you will accidentally feed the wrong wolf. I find that when I am struggling to start a project, or am stuck on a problem without being able to find a solution, I am feeding the wrong wolf. I am trapped in a cycle of fear or anxiety, or I am feeling down about myself.

Does that happen to you?

You
are
the CREATOR
of your
own
HAPPINESS.

When you think *I am not creative*, or *I cannot dance*, or *I am not going to get that promotion*, or whatever you might be thinking to downgrade yourself, you are starving the wolf that can bring you joy, peace, love, and happiness.

The words that you speak to yourself are powerful. When your brain says, "I cannot dance," it sends signals to your body, making it clumsier. These negative thoughts also create negative emotions, giving you less confidence.

Here is the good news: This feedback loop works both ways. When your brain says something positive, such as, "I think I am going to make a breakthrough soon!" you are much more likely to take a step forward toward your goal.

Consider how this affects your creative spirit. When you think your hobbies are silly or less important than all the other things on your plate, which wolf are you feeding? You are feeding the wolf that says you—and your interests—are not worthy of time. You give power to the evil wolf, which becomes stronger and stronger and eventually defeats the good wolf.

You are the master of those wolves. You are the creator of your own happiness. You get to decide which wolf wins by choosing which voices to listen to and which to proactively battle. Choose to focus on the good and let go of the bad. Keep in mind that each thought we have inside actually creates a flow of energy around us. It's important that we manifest the positive and productive thoughts.

To be clear, though, battling these wolves takes time and repetition. Having awareness of those voices, and the ways in which the evil wolf can inhibit your creativity, is the first step, but you need more than awareness. You need to consistently cultivate this mindfulness approach by changing your mindset and cultivating positive habits.

To give the good wolf strength, you must intentionally feed it, which at first takes conscientious effort. This is why that seemingly symbolic act of replacing negative thoughts with positive thoughts is so important. Your good wolf must be given a chance to grow stronger. Fortunately, we have, on average, about sixty thousand thoughts each day, so there is ample opportunity to practice. Over time, the practice of being mindful and intentional in an uplifting way will become habitual.

It's like learning to play the piano. At first, the process feels clumsy. When you are learning to play, your brain must be fully focused on making sure that your fingers reach the right keys. Even then, you stumble. Mastering a skill takes much repetition. Finally, after hundreds—maybe even thousands—of hours of practice, you can begin to play without full focus. Your fingers intuitively know which keys to reach for and you find your flow.

The same is true of feeding your wolves. If your good wolf is neglected, it will need more attention. You will need to focus on feeding your good wolf over and over. Your good wolf will become stronger than the evil wolf, and soon you will spend less time distracted by negativity; instead, you will choose the positive thought and move forward. You will learn to back away from fear and doubt. Turning your attention toward the uplifting emotions will allow for more light to shine on the potential for great outcomes.

CRAFT A LIFE YOU LOVE

When you are stuck, stop whatever you are doing and listen
to the words you are saying to yourself. What words are
you using? Are you feeding the evil wolf and starving the
good wolf?

Write those words down. See how they make you feel. (It
won't be pleasant.) Then, cross those words out in heavy
black ink! Use a colorful pencil or marker to replace them
with five positive actions, emotions, or truths that you
can claim in the place of those fears.

*I cannot dance might become I am learning how to dance,
I have patience, I am trying something new, I feel happy
when I listen to music, and I think I'm going to make a
breakthrough soon!*

right time, right place? rubbish!

———

Right out of college, I was working as a freelance fashion stylist, so I spent a lot of time outdoors on photo shoots. I needed to be able to pin clothes on the models, but I always had cold hands. Because I needed to work with my hands, gloves weren't the best option. I did what any crafter would do: I created my own solution. I crocheted some arm warmers to wear during photo shoots. I asked my mom to show me a basic stitch, and I whipped up a few pairs of what looked like sleeves with a thumb hole.

One day, I wore my arm warmers to an opening party for Blue Genes, a trendy denim boutique owned by three sisters. Blue Genes was fashion heaven: It was well curated with a mixture of up-and-coming labels paired with some better-known brands. A pair of jeans sold for around $200— and this was back in 2001.

I couldn't afford to buy anything, but while I was happily browsing, one of the owners of the store approached me.

"I love your arm warmers," she said. "Where did you get them?"

"I made them," I answered.

She asked me if she could place an order for the store!

I wanted to say, "I don't think I can manage that." I was nervous because I had just learned to crochet, and my time was limited: in addition to my work as a stylist, I was a hostess at a restaurant. Then I remembered that my incredibly supportive mom could help me, so I said yes.

I called my mom and asked her to fly from Chicago to Atlanta to help me fulfill the order. For the next few days, she and I sat together crocheting a dozen pairs of black and oatmeal arm warmers. It felt like a turning point in my career and, beyond that, I loved this time with my mom, just sitting and laughing and creating.

We dropped off the first shipment at Blue Genes on a Wednesday at 3:30 P.M. As I was standing there, a girl who was shopping bought a pair without even asking how much they cost.

My mom and I were thrilled. Three hours later, one of the owners called and said, "You're going to think we're crazy, but we sold out of half of them and need to order more."

What had started as a window-shopping trip turned into a business opportunity.

A few months later, I was dropping off an order outside of another boutique, and a photographer asked me if he could take some photos of me. He explained that his model had not arrived yet so he needed a stand-in, and I was wearing a cute outfit.

I felt nervous. I was not wearing makeup, and I had not showered. I was not usually on the other side of the camera, so I felt awkward. I did not *feel* like a model.

I said yes anyway.

The photographer posed me in front of a wall and shot my picture. A few months later, I grabbed the latest issue of *Lucky* magazine, and there I was!

This was back before blogs were popular, so magazines were a big deal. Models used tear sheets for their portfolios, meaning that they simply tore (or, more likely, cut) their pictures out of magazines and stuck them inside their portfolios.

I was not a model, but I was a struggling up-and-coming fashion stylist, so having that tear sheet to show people in my portfolio of fashion work was really neat, particularly because it was in *Lucky*, which, at the time, was the go-to fashion magazine. That tear sheet lent credibility to my name and my abilities.

I was lucky (pardon the pun).

But luck was only a small part of it. In a sense, I made my own luck. I was the creator of my own happiness. It wasn't just that I was in the right place at the right time. I realized that there were opportunities to feed my soul, *even though they made me nervous.*

What I learned is that, when something makes you nervous, that is your cue to say yes. Think about it: Are you ever nervous about things that do not matter to you? Nope. Never will you be nervous about washing the dishes. Never will you be nervous about that dead-end job for which you are overqualified. And never will you get butterflies in your stomach if you go on a date with someone with whom you feel no romantic connection.

Look around, and you will see no shortage of people who are plenty bright and plenty talented, but who are too scared to say yes. The people who are "lucky" are usually the ones who are willing to take a chance on opportunities that would make the average person too uncomfortable. We are not smarter or more talented than the rest of the world; we simply understand that feeling fearful means we are being beckoned in the direction of a big opportunity. Feeling nervous means that the thing we are being asked to do matters.

Most people get a case of the nerves and they quit even before they start. This is a self-sabotaging act. Their stomach begins to flutter and churn, and they want this feeling to go away.

But this feeling is a good thing! It might not *feel* good at the time, but it is an indicator that you should pay attention and bring your best self forward. It is your body's way of saying, "Do this. Your life matters."

Remember, you are the creator of your own happiness. It is up to you to know yourself, set goals, and to say yes when opportunities present themselves. Follow the uncertain path. Release the feelings of fear. Allow for growth and potential. You have the power to craft a life of significance, impact, and deep meaning.

CRAFT A LIFE YOU LOVE

Take a few minutes to reflect on a situation that makes you feel nervous. Then answer these questions:

Why does this situation make me feel uneasy?

_____

_____

_____

What is a goal that I have not yet accomplished?

_____

_____

_____

Does this situation further my goal or my life?

_____

_____

_____

What is one concrete action I can take this week as a step toward accomplishing this goal? (This can be as simple as telling a friend to hold you accountable, or doing research online.)

_____

_____

_____

_____

BREATHE. BELIEVE. RELEASE. RECEIVE.

the gift of evidence

────

When you begin to take control of creating your own happiness and owning your life, you will start seeing that the world is giving you support in the form of evidence all around you. Let me give you some examples from my personal and professional life.

One of the best presents I ever received was from one of my mentors. It was a gift certificate for a palm reader for my birthday. I had never experienced a palm reading before and, while I admit I was a bit skeptical, it did seem like it would be fun and entertaining. I appreciated the gift, but I assumed it would ultimately represent something a little bit offbeat and absurd that I did before going about my life as usual.

Because the palm reader was in another state, our session had to be conducted over the phone. I giggled as I put my hands on a copy machine and mailed the black-and-white copies of my palms to her, as she instructed. We scheduled the call after she received my photocopies.

Turns out, having the hour-long palm-reading session was an important part of my journey. I'll never forget what she said to me when we started: "You have creative hands. You are going to do something big with them."

I was in my early twenties at the time, and I was just getting started in my career. I had already survived some threats to my creative path, and I had a few roadblocks ahead of me.

When the palm reader told me I had creative hands, the air actually left my chest. I felt a little light-headed. It was as though the Universe were backing me up, saying, "You go, girl!"

I wrote down everything she said in a journal that I uncovered many years later. Looking back, much of what she said to me turned out to be true. She told me things that were both good and bad—for instance, that I had a lot of angels watching over me, but that I wouldn't really feel settled until my thirties. She said I was strong and adaptable, and that would help guide me.

I have no idea how she was able to read these things from those photocopies, but what I do know for certain is that she gave me some evidence that I was on the right path at a time when I needed proof.

Later, when I encountered more obstacles, I remembered what the palm reader told me, and it motivated me to keep going. When I found that journal, it further inspired me to draw upon my innate strength and adaptability once again.

I have had other signs from the Universe along the way. Once I found myself sitting next to supermodel Cindy Crawford at a blackjack table at the opening of the Green Valley Resort in Las Vegas. Nothing transpired between us, but it is hard *not* to notice someone as stunning as Cindy Crawford. I do not get starstruck easily, but that moment was ingrained into my memory because she seemed like such a beautiful person, inside and out.

And guess what? Several months later, a friend and store owner called to let me know that Cindy Crawford was photographed in *Glamour* magazine wearing one of my hand-embroidered tank tops! She was photographed by paparazzi doing leg lifts and looking amazing in one of the pieces my mom and I had created by hand.

I took those two experiences as further evidence of the synchronicity between me and the Universe: "Keep creating, Amy. Keep creating."

This is how these stories apply to you: You are going to face challenges. Things are going to derail you from your goals. Open yourself to finding evidence that you are on the right path. Even if it seems silly at the time (like photocopying your palms), tuck it into your memory and string the pieces of proof together to remind yourself that you are heading in the right direction.

CRAFT A LIFE YOU LOVE

Curtis Estes, a friend of my partner, JC, discusses something called a "Highlight Reel" in his book *Your Life By Design*. Curtis's Highlight Reel consists of "the biggest and boldest moments of our lives, the memories that carry spiritual and emotional sustenance."

My take on this concept is called an "Evidence Reel." My Evidence Reel is a running list of all the evidence the Universe has given me to tell me that I am on the right path. Here, you'll create your own Evidence Reel: It will consist not just of the signs that you have been given, but also the signs that you have given yourself. It includes all of the accomplishments and the milestones you have already achieved.

> **"If a person measures success by looking at the distances she has yet to travel, she will always be disappointed. If, on the other hand, she measures success by the distance she has already traveled, she will see that she has already reached great success."**
>
> —CURTIS ESTES

Creating an Evidence Reel helps us to feed the good wolf. It tells us we are on the right path, that we have momentum, and that we are in synchronicity with the Universe. In times of difficulty, it reminds us that we are the creators of our own happiness. Just as scrapbooking is proof of a good life, so too is an Evidence Reel. It allows you to focus on your successes, reinforcing the idea that your life matters and has meaning.

My Evidence Reel:

_____

_____

_____

_____

_____

_____

_____

_____

_____

_____

_____

_____

_____

_____

_____

_____

_____

_____

be grateful for everything
you do not have

———

Tony Robbins has a concept that I love. It's called "blaming elegantly." The idea is this: If everyone in your life behaved exactly the way you wanted him or her to behave, you would not be the person you are today. So if you are going to blame people for everything that has gone wrong, blame them for all the lessons you learned by watching them do whatever it was that you didn't want them to do.

If you are going to blame your mother for being too critical, you also have to blame her for your reaction that developed your remarkable compassion. If you are going to blame your father for being cold and distant, you have to blame him for the fact that, as a result, you sought out and married someone who is ever-present, warm, and loving. If you are going to blame your boss for your dead-end job, you have to blame her for creating a situation where you gained insight into what lights your soul.

In other words, recognize people for who they are, learn from their flaws, and be grateful to them for all of the lessons you learned and the blessings you received because of them.

I value this idea because I never want resentment to stand in the way of feeling joyful and carefree. I don't want my life to be chained to someone else's failures. I want to know, without a doubt, that I am brave, bold, and unshackled by my history. I want to remember that I am the creator of my own happiness, and that my happiness is not beholden to someone else's behavior.

When you blame elegantly, something marvelous happens: You will have an easier time forgiving the people in your life, and the heavy weight of anger and resentment will become lighter and lighter. You will learn to let go.

A corollary of blaming elegantly is the idea of being grateful for everything that you *don't* have. So often, we want what other people have. We feel a twinge of jealousy because they were blessed with more money, better looks, or more talent. We fail to consider what we would lose if we had those things.

I used to want a mansion and a ten-car garage for my SUV, my convertible, and all of the other cars that I thought I wanted. I thought having loads of money would bring me happiness. Maybe it would, but maybe it would also mean that I had to work longer hours and endure more stress—more investments to worry about, more people whose salaries I had to pay, more belongings that need to be protected—and less time with my son and partner, time that I cherish.

So, instead of having the constant desire for the big things that I don't have, I try to focus on feeling grateful for the little things that I do have, which add up to the big things that matter most: the weekends I have with my family, the weekdays I can snuggle with Jack because of a flexible schedule that allows me time to spend with him, and the simple lifestyle that allows me time to focus on all the things that are most important to me: my family, my career, my health, and my hobbies.

I am reminded of the story of the Mexican fisherman. One day, a fisherman pulled up to a dock and struck up a conversation with an American businessman who was vacationing in Mexico. The businessman complimented the fisherman on his catches for the day.

"It is still early in the day," said the businessman. "Are you going back out to catch more fish?"

"No," replied the fisherman, "I have all I need to feed my family."

"What are you going to do with the rest of your day?" asked the businessman.

"I'm going to play with my children, take a nap with my wife, play my

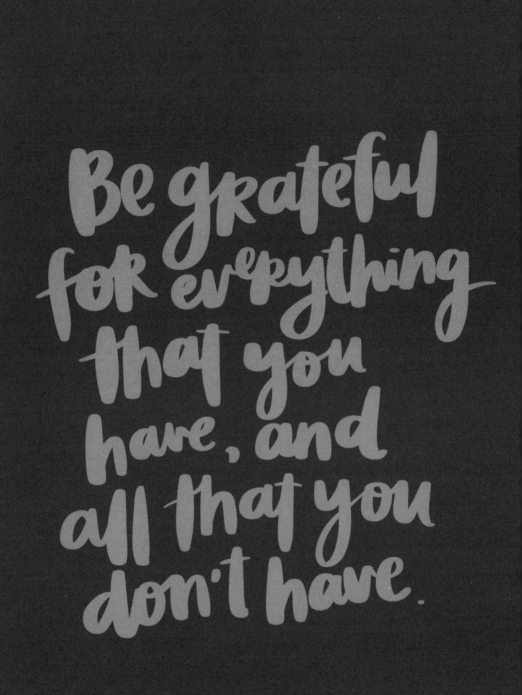

Be grateful for everything that you have, and all that you don't have.

guitar a little, sip some wine, and walk into the village and eat dinner with my family," replied the fisherman.

The businessman said, "If you spent only a couple more hours a day catching fish, you could sell the extra fish and buy a bigger boat so that you can catch more fish. With that income, you could buy a second boat and hire someone to help you. Then buy a third boat, and so on until you have an entire fleet of fishing boats."

"Then what?" asked the fisherman.

"Eventually, you could sell your fishing business and make a ton of money."

"What would I do with the money?" asked the fisherman.

The businessman's reply was this: "Retire and move to a coastal village. Play with your children, take naps with your wife, strum on your guitar, and enjoy leisurely dinners with your family."

CRAFT A LIFE YOU LOVE

Crafting your own happiness means that you take control
of your mindset.

What are some of the ways you can reframe your thoughts
so that you practice gratitude around the things you
do *not* have? Perhaps you wish that you had more money,
a partner who gave you more attention, or a sleeveless,
bright aqua blue dress with a choker collar, and a fit
that hugs the waist and hips and flares at the knees like
a mermaid's tail.

Choose one thing you wish you had and make a list of
pros and cons.

Here is something I do not have:

_____

_____

Cons:

_____

_____

_____

_____

_____

_____

_____

Pros:

_____

_____

_____

_____

_____

I am grateful that I do not have this because:

_____

_____

_____

_____

_____

Lessons I have learned as a result:

_____

_____

_____

_____

_____

_____

i will not complain.
i will not complain.
i will not complain.

———

If you let yourself, you can likely find quite a few things to complain about—and some of those complaints are probably valid. But think about this: Every time you complain, you are simultaneously eliminating an opportunity to think about something positive and fulfilling. You are letting negativity take hold of a moment that might otherwise be just great.

When I was ten years old, I made a New Year's resolution to keep my room clean, and I promptly shared my resolution with everyone in my family. (In case you are wondering, I failed miserably at this resolution, which lasted about three days.)

At any rate, I remember asking my dad what resolution he had, and he confessed that he had not set a specific New Year's resolution.

"Why not?" I asked him. For a ten-year-old kid, failing to set a New Year's resolution seemed a little bit blasphemous.

"I try to set resolutions all year 'round," he told me.

Twenty-four years later, when my son, Jack, was born, that conversation came back to me. I want to give him the best I can, so, all year 'round, I resolve to become a better person and a kinder, more patient mother. My love for Jack motivates me to make changes so that I can give him the best of myself. Sometimes the changes are sweeping, but most of the time, they are gradual. They happen a little bit at a time, day by day.

Then I was summoned for jury duty four times over the course of eighteen months. Surely, the Universe was trying to tell me something (or maybe the Los Angeles Superior Court was simply asking me to do my civic duty). Regardless, I had been given an opportunity to make a huge change in my mindset.

The first time I was summoned for jury duty, I was nine months pregnant and expecting Jack any day. I did not want to go into labor in a courtroom—and I doubted anyone else wanted that either—so I requested an extension. I received my second summons when Jack was five months old. I was still nursing, so I requested another extension. Then I requested another extension when I received my third summons six months later and was still nursing Jack.

When I received my fourth summons, I was out of options. I had to go into the courthouse.

I woke on my first morning of jury duty, and I have to confess that the idea of missing work to sit in a room of strangers was unappealing. I believe in our jury system, and if I were ever on trial, I would want a fair, impartial jury of my peers to judge me. Still, like most people, I was feeling irritated and frustrated about being pulled out of my routine.

I looked in the mirror, feeling grumpy, and I reminded myself that every day, I have an opportunity to be a better person. I realized that I want Jack to have a mom who is optimistic and who can roll with the punches. I decided to feed the good wolf and create my own happiness.

Then and there, I resolved: "I will not complain for the next twenty-four hours."

On any given day, this is a tough resolution to master, much less on a day spent in a crowded downtown Los Angeles courtroom full of people who would sooner cliff dive into shark-infested waters than fulfill their civic duty.

Still, I figured that if I could pull it off on this day, I could do it any day, so I went about packing my bag. I took two books, a blank journal, and my traveler's notebook. I noticed right away that I was intentionally leaving some things behind—namely, my laptop. I was unsure of whether the courtroom would have Wi-Fi, and I did not want to feel aggravated. I wanted to set myself up for success, so I left all possible frustrations at home.

My resolve was challenged within ten minutes of arriving at the courthouse. I found myself seated next to a gentleman who was talking on the phone—loudly. I started to think about how difficult it was to read while listening to his conversation, but then I stopped and replaced that thought. I thought, *This is an opportunity to listen to some music.* So I put my headphones in and relaxed.

The room was packed with people who were cranky. I overheard more than a few people's complaints, but every time my mind started to wander to something negative, I forced myself to think something positive.

I'm uncomfortable turned into *I should get up and walk around and check out those magazines over there.*

That lady is being so rude turned into *I am so glad that I have the ability to tune people out so that I can read.*

Every time I started to complain, I forced a new thought into my head, such as *What can I do to make this a great day?*

A few hours into the day, I noticed something: I was no longer making an effort to have positive thoughts. They were coming naturally. In fact, more than once, I thought about how great it was to just sit and do nothing. I had a sixteen-month-old son at home, so just sitting felt like a luxury.

We had a lunch break from 11:30 A.M. to 12:30 P.M., so I texted my friend Jamie to see if she could have lunch with me. She picked me up; we went to one of her favorite lunch spots, which is now one of my favorite lunch spots; and she took me back to the courthouse.

That afternoon, I learned that I would have to return the next day, but you know what? That was okay with me. I was not nearly as irritated as most of the other jurors.

Since I was already downtown, I decided to go to the fabric district and pick up some fabric. While I was there, I connected with a friend who invited me to meet her for dinner at the Lexus Club and then attend the Clippers game. I stumbled upon a boutique that had the perfect Clippers-blue dress and necklace. Happily, I made the purchase and walked out of the store wearing my new outfit.

We ended up with spectacular seats, just a few rows behind Jay-Z and Beyoncé.

When I finally made it home, I realized that I had had a blast that day. I connected with some friends, saw a basketball game, had a celebrity sighting, read a great book, relaxed, and fed my creative soul (I love fabric stores).

It bears repeating: You are the creator of your own happiness. You get to decide which thoughts to focus on and which ones to replace. You get to decide whether you will allow grumpy thoughts to remain in your head or whether you will actively and intentionally work to replace them with thoughts that make you feel joyful.

CRAFT A LIFE YOU LOVE

Take a few minutes to actively and intentionally work to replace complaints with thoughts that make you feel happy.

What are some of the things I complain about on a regular basis?

_____

_____

_____

I am frustrated about _____ ,
but if I think about it another way, I can see that
it is actually an opportunity for me to

_____

_____

_____ .

Here are a few times when something great ended up coming out of something challenging:

1. _____

2. _____

3. _____

Remember: You are the creator of your own happiness, and you get to decide which thoughts to focus on.

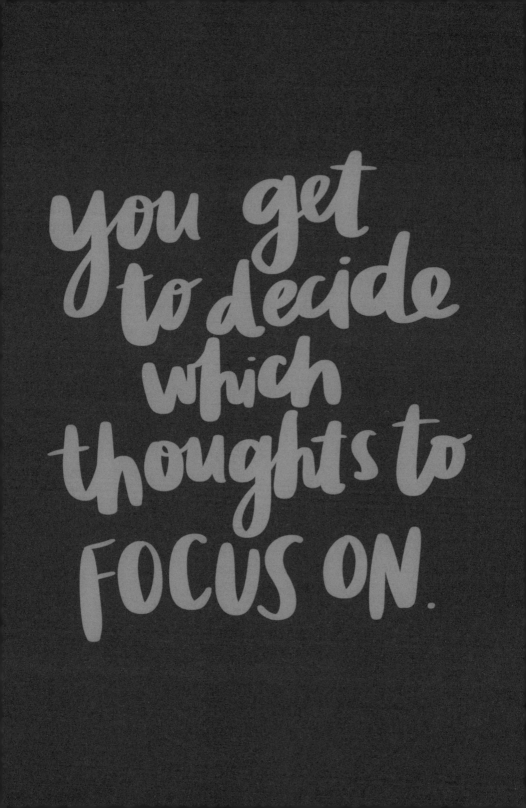

crafting the **RIGHT** **ENVIRONMENT**

you're gonna need a bigger boat

─────

In the movie *Jaws*, there's a scene where Chief Brody (Roy Scheider) is in a tiny fishing boat with Quint, a grizzled shark hunter, trying to capture the shark. Brody sees the three-ton, twenty-five-foot great white shark for the first time. Stunned at the shark's size, he backs into the cabin of the boat and, with a cigarette still dangling from his mouth, says, "You're gonna need a bigger boat."

That scene got me thinking about the importance of my "boat." By this, I mean my surroundings and all of the tools I use to make sure that I can have space—physically and mentally—to bring what I want and need into my life and to accomplish my goals.

Specifically, there are three things that go into making an adequate boat:

1. Physical environment
2. Mindset
3. People

PHYSICAL ENVIRONMENT

At any given time, I have a dozen or so projects going on. I'm currently working on cool new creative collaborations, making and posting YouTube videos on my channel twice a week, and renovating my studio—not to mention writing this book! All of the fabric and yarn and paper could easily take over my home.

But I have learned that the fewer things that are competing for my attention at any given time, the more I am able to focus on the creative work at hand. I cannot tackle designing products, making videos, and organizing my studio all at once, so I intentionally choose one project to work on at a time, and keep supplies for all of the others contained and out of my line of vision. I also cannot answer phone calls or respond to text messages *and* be fully "in the zone," so I often keep my computer and my phone away from me while I am working on projects. By keeping my surroundings simple, I am able to give each project the full attention it deserves when I am ready to work on it.

I have also found that this makes me a better mother and a better partner. When I keep my surroundings simple, nothing competes with my family for my attention. Instead of being distracted by piles of unfinished creations, I can be Jack's mom and I can enjoy JC's company, fully present and at ease in my surroundings.

Pay attention to your physical environment: It will either be a distraction, or it will energize you. Reducing clutter is a good way to make your boat big enough—so, too, is creating a space that is beautiful and inspiring.

Another way to create an environment that energizes you is by creating a mood board that lives somewhere in the vicinity of your crafting area. You have probably heard of a vision board, which is a big poster or a bulletin board with pictures representing all the goals that you want to accomplish. A mood board is similar to a vision board, but it represents the mood that you want to create. Because your mood is such an important part of your ability to create, protecting it and feeding it are essential to creating an environment for success.

When you come across something that moves you, print it out or make a copy of it and put it on your mood board. This might be a quote, a picture, or even a memento. Whatever is on your mood board will serve as a tangible reminder of the positive emotions that you want to feel at all times.

I struggle with anxiety, so my mood board is filled with enlightening quotes and serene pictures that remind me to be calm. There are also pictures of my favorite moments with Jack and JC, reminding me of the love and joy that they bring to my life. When I am feeling anxious, I take five minutes to meditate in front of my mood board. This small but simple act goes a long way toward making sure that my physical environment feeds my soul.

MINDSET

Your mind also needs to be a "big enough boat." It is important to give everything that is on your mind a place. Be intentional about when you think about things, work on them, or deal with them.

I have a rule that if something pops up and can be dealt with in fewer than five minutes, I do it right then and there. For instance, when I book travel, I immediately put all the details into my calendar with the appropriate notes and alarms. If I know I have to write a brief but tough email, I do it immediately. This saves a lot of future hassle: Instead of adding it to my list of things to do, it is taken care of on the spot while I am still thinking about it. Putting off things that would add to my list of worries is silly and counterproductive.

If the task will take more than five minutes, I give it a time slot in my schedule. If I simply add it to my to-do list without assigning time to accomplish it, I feel a little bit of anxiety about getting everything done. If, instead, I give everything on my mind a time to be addressed, then I know that I will have time for everything on my list. Of course, there are many times I have underestimated how long it takes to do things (I still do this!), but that error only reinforces the importance of scheduling time—accurately.

This is one of the big reasons that I suggest that you set aside a time to journal every day. This time is an appointment with yourself, one that serves to address all of your concerns, aspirations, and goals. When you find your mind drifting during the day, remind yourself that you will have time to address whatever is worrying you during your journaling time. Putting pen to paper (or even fingers to keyboard) helps to bring clarity and focus. You must make time for the things that are important to you, and when you do, this will help in freeing your mind of worry and fear.

PEOPLE

This is a big one! Do the people in your life fill you with joy and energy? If so, make sure to make time for them. You will always be more motivated and more productive when you are surrounded by people who have big dreams and empower you to think optimistically about your future.

Of course, the reverse is also true: When people in your life cause unnecessary drama, you will have a hard time getting anything done. Worrying about people who don't bring you joy takes up valuable brain space. This is your cue to build a bigger boat to accommodate the people who value you, and to draw boundaries and be clear about how you feel when you are around people who don't. You will not always be able to distance yourself from people who suck your energy, but you can always take intentional steps to be a little more conscientious about the people in your boat.

CRAFT A LIFE YOU LOVE

Have you ever considered the three things you would take
to a deserted island? Let's put a spin on this exercise.
Instead, consider who and what you need inside your boat
in order to get to that island. In other words, what do
you need to set yourself up for reaching your goals?

Consider all of the aspects we discussed: your physical
environment, your mindset, and the people you want to
accompany you along the way. Then, make a list below of
your boat's physical characteristics, describe how you
feel when you are aboard, and list the people who have
joined you on the journey.

_____

_____

_____

_____

_____

_____

_____

_____

_____

_____

_____

_____

Eliminate those things that do not matter.

(Make time for what matters most.)

YOU CAN DO IT!

you have enough time

—

My very smart friend Elise declared that she was going to stop saying, "I don't have enough time." Instead, she reframed her thinking and belief to: "I have enough time for everything that matters to me."

I value her declaration for two reasons: First, saying "I have enough time" feeds the good wolf. It feels optimistic and achievable. It opens the window of opportunity. When you tell the Universe that you do not have enough time, you create a negative feedback loop. You feel anxious and nervous and guilty for all the things you do not have time to accomplish, and feeling this way almost guarantees that you will behave this way. Instead of being relaxed and efficient, you will be uptight.

When you say, "I have enough time," you feel confident. You can go about your days feeling at peace and in the moment. You can minimize worrying about the future, knowing that you do have enough time to get the most important things done.

But, more important, deciding that you have enough time *for everything that matters* forces you to prioritize and eliminate those things that do not matter. If you let *time* dictate how you spend your days, you will simply say yes to the first people who ask you for your time, and you will say no to the last people who ask you for your time. This is no way to live!

When you say, "I don't have time," you are telling the world and yourself that you are being controlled by outside forces—that your choices are dictated by a clock that controls how you move through a life determined by to-dos. Only after you mark one item off your to-do list will you have time for the next person or activity or goal.

Stephen Covey, author of *The 7 Habits of Highly Effective People*, tells the story of putting rocks, gravel, and sand inside a jar. If you start filling the jar randomly, you will probably not be able to fit all of the big rocks inside. But if you start with the big rocks, then the gravel, then the sand, all of the big rocks are more likely to fit. This story is a reminder to say yes to the big things. You have enough time. In fact, when time stops being the dictator, you can replace it with a far more effective method of determining when you say no and when you say yes.

When you start being intentional about how you spend your time, paying close attention to what matters and what does not matter, you begin to realize the opportunity cost associated with each decision. You see, time is never the real problem. Time is a fixed asset for everyone. The real problem is that every *yes* is a *no* to something else.

When you say yes to joining the Halloween Decorating Committee at your child's school simply because you feel guilty and you think you should spend some time volunteering, you are simultaneously saying no to all the other things you could be doing, such as working on your craft. When you say yes to watching a television show instead of going to sleep, you are simultaneously saying no to waking up early so that you can practice yoga.

> **"Time is really the only capital that any human being has, and the only thing he can't afford to lose."**
> —THOMAS EDISON

CRAFT A LIFE YOU LOVE

Track how you spend each hour of the day for two days.

_____

_____

_____

_____

_____

_____

_____

_____

_____

_____

_____

_____

_____

_____

_____

_____

_____

How are you spending your time? How much time did you spend on the "big rocks" (i.e., your highest priorities)?

_____

_____

_____

_____

_____

_____

_____

_____

_____

_____

_____

_____

_____

_____

_____

Now, create an ideal schedule by putting in your highest priorities and non-negotiables first. Then fit in your smaller obligations and responsibilities.

_____

_____

_____

_____

_____

_____

_____

_____

_____

_____

_____

_____

_____

_____

_____

_____

_____

_____

Remember: If you are clear on the priorities in your life, you will find time for everything that matters. The trick is identifying and prioritizing the things that matter.

You can do this by asking yourself the one question . . .

the one question

——

There is one question that I believe every creator needs to ask before making a decision. I'll tell you what that one question is momentarily, but first I want to tell you a two-part story.

I started my career in fashion. When I was twenty-two years old, I took my first T-shirt collection to a four-day trade show in New York. The cost of the trade show, plus expenses, added up to $10,000, so my goal was to sell $20,000 worth of product during the four days of the event. Essentially, I thought that this goal would help recoup my costs so I could spend the next few months fulfilling the orders.

I didn't sell $20,000 worth of product in four days. I sold $20,000 the *first day* of the show. By day four, I had orders totaling $50,000.

I was ecstatic.

But soon thereafter, I was overwhelmed. Not only did I have to figure out a way to make all of the hand-stitched T-shirts, but I also had to handle all of the back-end administrative work, such as boxing up and shipping out orders. My main concern was getting the product produced locally.

I lived in Atlanta at the time, and by word-of-mouth and a little luck, I found some great hand sewers. My cleaning lady had several friends who lived in her apartment complex who loved to sew. I interviewed them, and it turned out they were far more skilled than I was, not to mention much faster at putting the T-shirts together.

I found myself working around the clock to keep production moving. I was "upcycling" men's T-shirts by cutting them into women's silhouettes and drawing a design on the front. I carefully hand-cut everything, which took quite a bit of time.

It was a long process to make the shirts and, because it involved special techniques, I accepted help only with stitching. There were many other tasks involved, but I did not think I had the time to train others properly.

Months later, it was time to ship. The first lot left smoothly, but then I became inundated with the tasks of invoicing and keeping track of finances.

When it was time to ship the second batch, I had not completed half of the order. During a time in my career when $20 was a lot of money, I lost about $20,000.

At the time, it stung. I was deeply disappointed in myself for not working harder. In retrospect, this was the beginning of a two-part lesson, the first of which is this: You cannot protect the days, weeks, months, and years of your life if you do not protect the minutes of your life. You see, I could have and should have delegated many tasks. The women who worked so hard at hand-stitching could have helped with cutting. It would have cost me only $2,000 to hire a full-time employee to help with all of the administrative and fulfillment tasks.

Instead, I took everything on. I wanted to be Superwoman, so I tried to do it all.

I am not Superwoman, so I failed.

I lost more than money: I lost some key relationships with buyers and, most of all, I lost the ability to feed my soul. I could have spent those months creating, but I spent the days rushing around doing things other people could have easily helped me with. I was so busy trying to do it all that I lost the opportunity to do the thing I love most—creating.

The second part of this lesson happened years later, when I was living in Los Angeles. Again, my business took off: I was selling about $100,000 worth of product most months. I had a few employees, and I was building a name for my little business. Because I was working in an industry that seemed creative, I figured that I should be thrilled and fulfilled because I was doing what I loved to do, at least on paper.

The truth is, though, that I felt a lot of pressure. Coming up with new ideas and collections in the fast-paced fashion industry was exhausting. Though I had systems in place to help me, I felt like I was always chasing something that could not be caught. I spent about only 5 percent of my time designing, which was my passion. I was working from the moment I woke up until the time I went to sleep. The weekends were full of work, too, and I didn't take an actual vacation for years. I felt burnt out. It was just too much for me to handle. So, instead of feeding my soul, my fashion line was depleting all of my reserves.

Then one day, on the way to my mom's house, I walked into a scrapbook store. I had driven by the store countless times before, but something made me stop and walk in. I noticed a sign for a scrapbooking workshop the next day.

I decided to sign up for the class, and this decision changed my life. During the class, as I was cutting paper, applying stickers, and choosing embellishments, I felt my spirit get lighter and my mood get brighter. The passion that I had always felt when I was creating returned. I needed that feeling. Hand-stitching T-shirts had provided it before, but I realized that it no longer did. I knew my focus was shifting away from the fashion industry and into something fresh and new.

This change in focus happens in all areas of life, not just with business. You might start off loving something or someone, but then life changes, and the way that those things evolve ends up pulling you away from what attracted you to them in the first place. Maybe you love being a mom, but then you spend so much time running errands, cooking, and cleaning that you do not actually get to parent your children. Maybe you love your partner, but you spend so much time bickering that you no longer sit around laughing. Or maybe you loved your job, but now you are spending only 5 percent of your time doing the parts that you truly enjoy.

Here is the truth: Minutes become hours, which become days, which become weeks, which become months, which become years. How you spend your minutes determines how you spend your years. So, if you are not careful, minutes will slowly join together to form weeks and years of your life that do not represent your heart's desires or needs. Just fifteen minutes a day equals one workday a month! If you treat the minutes of your life with care and respect, you will simultaneously protect the years of your life.

> **When you know what's important, it's a lot easier to ignore what's not.**
> —MARIE FORLEO

So how do you make sure that you protect your minutes? I have found that it starts by asking one simple question: **"Does this activity feed my soul?"**

Does being head of the PTA feed your soul? Depending on who you are, it might do just that. Perhaps you love the camaraderie, or perhaps your position allows you to feel as if you are part of the working world at a time when your career is on pause so that you can raise your children. But for others, being head of the PTA might feel like a time suck. It might not feed your soul.

Only you can decide this, but one thing is certain: If you do not conscientiously take charge of the minutes of your life, they will slip through your fingers. Focus on what is important, prioritize those things, and optimize your windows of time.

CRAFT A LIFE YOU LOVE

Look at the list of all of the ways you spend your time from page 86. For each activity, ask yourself, "Does this feed my soul?"

If the answer is no, think of all the creative ways that you can delegate or work toward removing this item from your list of responsibilities. For example, when Jack was a newborn, I decided I would rather spend quality time with him instead of scrubbing my toilets. Delegating the task of cleaning my house was well worth the money we spent on it. Baby cuddles last only a short time!

ACTIVITY	CREATIVE WAYS TO DELEGATE OR ELIMINATE

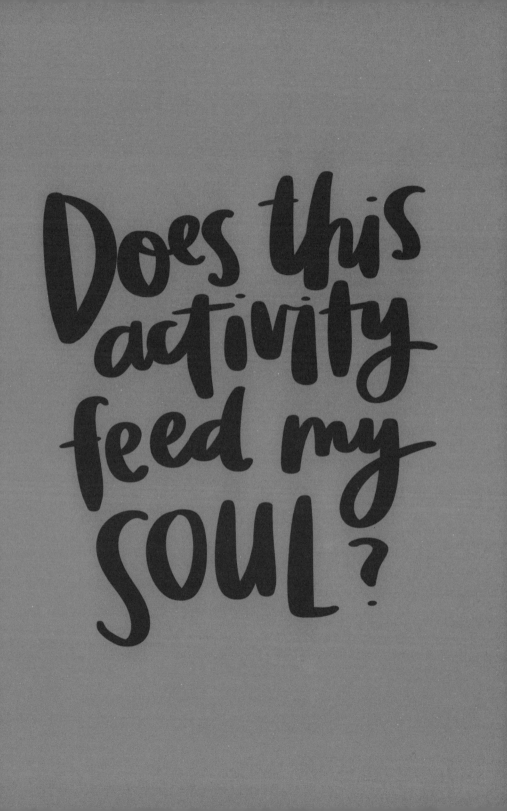

the rule of positivity

—

If you throw something positive into the Universe, it will respond with something as good as or better than what you wished for. The Universe cannot help itself. It is naturally benevolent. The powers that be—and all of the people who love you—want you to succeed. They want your dreams to come true.

Too often, we are afraid of saying what we want. Whether it is a dream relationship, a dream job, or a dream vacation, we might feel that saying it aloud makes us vulnerable, and we are ashamed to admit our desires. If we say it aloud, then what happens if we don't achieve it? How embarrassing!

The Universe does not work like that, though. Positivity begets positivity. Just look around: Happy, optimistic people attract other happy, optimistic people. Inspiring people attract inspiring people, and when you throw goodness into the world, you will attract goodness.

So, with a pure heart, ask the powers that be to help you make your dreams come true—and be specific.

I know a guy who sent an email to all his friends asking them to introduce him to women. He said he wanted to get married and have a "whole team" of children. He described what he wanted in his future wife, and he offered to write a $10,000 check to the person who introduced him to her.

Do you think sending that email was easy for him? I imagine that he felt a little bit raw and silly. He was probably embarrassed, and he certainly knew that he risked public humiliation. But his intentions were good: He wanted to find love, and he sent that email into a world filled with people who also wanted him to find love.

Today he is married and has five children.

Here is another example: Shortly after I started scrapbooking, I was at a happy hour with Gillian, a dear friend of mine, and I said, "Wouldn't it be great if I had just one awesome client I could scrapbook for consistently?"

Getting paid to scrapbook someone else's memories seemed a little absurd to me, but I was beginning to tire of documenting my own memories. I had just gotten out of a long-term relationship and could only scrapbook so much about my Jack Russell terriers. Scrapbooking was my creative outlet, and my intentions were pure, so I asked the question.

Gillian said, "I think I know someone."

She introduced me to a woman who has seven children. That incredible woman has hired me to scrapbook all her children's birthdays, bar mitzvahs and bat mitzvahs, trips across the world, and school functions. She has been a client for nine years.

That happy-hour conversation represented a turning point in my scrapbooking business. If I had been too ashamed to say something out loud to my friend, I would not have had the opportunity to meet this amazing family who has enabled me to do what I love on a daily basis.

My client roster has grown since then, but starting with one person was all it took. We have regular work from wonderful clients all over the country, and I am able to employ other scrapbookers who can use their talents and work from home on these projects. The collaborative memory albums are handcrafted, treasured keepsakes.

It makes sense that your dreams are infinitely more likely to come true when you are backed by all the powerful forces of the Universe. Give it a try. Throw something wild and wonderful out there. See how good things begin to happen with each step you take.

CRAFT A LIFE YOU LOVE

Here is an exercise I'm borrowing from my friend Melissa
for creating something new for yourself, whether it is
a career, a family, or a habit.

On page 99, draw a heart to signify the love that you
are putting into the Universe.

In the middle of the heart, write: "I AM."

Draw rays coming out from the heart. On each ray, write
down a positive thing that you currently enjoy doing or
want to be doing.

At the top of the page, write, "This or something
better, for the highest good of all concerned."

Look at this every chance that you get.
Read it out loud.

At first, you might simply whisper it to yourself.
You might feel too vulnerable to say it to friends
and acquaintances, and that is okay. Just speak
it, and allow it seep into your soul. Then, when you
feel comfortable, speak it to your closest friend,
and then to another friend. By expressing the love
and joy that you want to create, you will witness the
Universe beginning to respond, providing you with
what you have asked for, or something better. Whatever
happens next, remember to add it to your Evidence
Reel (see page 60)!

this OR something better for the highest good of all concerned.

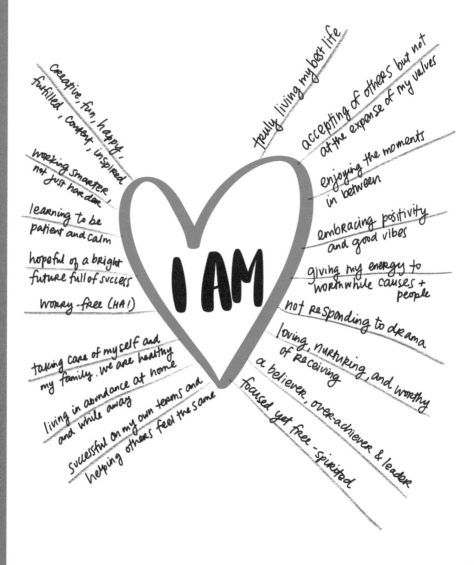

truly living my best life

accepting of others but not at the expense of my values

enjoying the moments in between

embracing positivity and good vibes

giving my energy to worthwhile causes + people

not responding to drama

loving, nurturing, and worthy of receiving

a believer, over-achiever & leader

focused yet free-spirited

I AM

creative, fun, happy, fulfilled, content, inspired

working smarter, not just harder

learning to be patient and calm

hopeful of a bright future full of success

worry-free (HA!)

taking care of myself and my family. we are healthy

living in abundance at home and while away

successful on my own terms and helping others feel the same

willpower

A lot of people believe that willpower is either something you have or something you do not have. They think, *Oh, I don't have the willpower.* Maybe even *you* have said this before. (This is your evil wolf talking, by the way.)

But I don't believe that willpower is an innate trait that some people have and others lack. *Everyone* has willpower. The difference is that some people cultivate their willpower and some people do not. People who have "more willpower" actually do not have *more* of anything other than practice. They have practiced making the same choice so many times that the choice appears to be second nature.

Let's say that you wake up in the morning and think, *Today I am going to spend thirty minutes working on my craft. No matter what happens, I am going to carve out thirty minutes to spend doing what I love.*

Then your day goes haywire. Your son's teacher calls and says that you have to come pick him up from school because he is sick. All of a sudden, the time you had blocked out midmorning to work on your craft is spent driving to and from your son's school. Your errands, the work you had to accomplish, the gym session—they are all pushed to the back burner because, of course, your son comes first.

Now your thought is, *I don't have time to work on my craft.*

If you do not have experience cultivating your willpower, this might be the end of your internal conversation. The day will end without your taking the time to work on the intention you set in the morning.

But if you decide that you are going to start cultivating your willpower, can you guess what you will do? You will force your brain to replace this thought with another one: *Even though my schedule has been interrupted, I am going to make it a priority and find the time to work on my craft.* You still have the same initial thought (*I don't have the time to work on my craft*), but you intentionally replace it with a thought that strengthens your willpower.

Perhaps this seems overly simplistic, but give it a try. Let's say that you decide that instead of spending time on social media sites, you are going to dedicate that time to your craft. Then you get frustrated or bored with your project, and you think, *I wonder what is happening on Instagram.*

As soon as you are aware of a thought that will not serve your goal, choose to replace it with something else, over and over and over: *I am going to work on my craft instead. I am going to work on my craft instead. I am going to work on my craft instead.*

If you force your brain to repeat this same thought, you *will* work on your craft. You see, your thoughts greatly influence your behavior. When you begin focusing on high-level thoughts, your energy and actions will flow in the right direction. Eventually, the thoughts will become second nature, and so will the behavior.

Thoughts and feelings fuel actions. Think good thoughts and do good things.

> **❝Our thoughts create our lives, but it's not just as easy as thinking about something. Our thoughts create our feelings and our actions, therefore our actions create our results.❞**
> —BROOKE CASTILLO

CRAFT A LIFE YOU LOVE

How can you begin to cultivate your willpower through practice? Remember, if you force your brain to repeat the same thought over and over, you will develop strength, and you will become increasingly in control of your thoughts, actions, and emotions.

When do I feel my crafting willpower is low?

_____

_____

What motivating thoughts can I focus on in these situations?

_____

_____

When do I feel out of control with respect to my time with my craft?

_____

_____

What small steps can I take to gain some control?

_____

_____

_____

_____

_____

_____

Thoughts
and feelings
fuel actions.

THINK GOOD
THOUGHTS and
DO GOOD THINGS.

crafting happiness
THROUGH HABITS

turning happiness into a habit

O ne of the most startling statistics that I read recently is from *The Power of Full Engagement,* a book by Jim Loehr and Tony Schwartz. According to the book, up to 95 percent of our life is based on habits. My first thought was, *That can't be true,* but the more I thought about it, the more it made sense. We usually wake up at the same time; we brush our teeth, shower, dress, and eat breakfast in approximately the same manner; we take the same route to work.

These kinds of habits can affect whether or not we are happy. If we love our habits, we generally love our lives. Likewise, if our habits are boring or unfulfilling, we can feel bored and unfulfilled. (I am not talking about brushing your teeth before you go to bed, although I have tried to make that process more fun by doing leg lifts and squats while my Sonicare does its thing.)

A big theme of this book, in fact, is that making a habit of practicing your hobbies will go a long way toward nourishing your soul. You cannot be happy if you are not habitually engaging in side projects that you love doing.

This section covers practical tips that you can use to create habits surrounding your craft so that your life is filled with love, happiness, and fulfillment. Before we look at these practical tips, let's talk about making happiness a habit.

While it is true that you always have a choice—you have a choice about where to spend your time and your energy, you have a choice about which wolf you will feed, you have a choice about whether you will complain or whether you will feel grateful—it is also true that converting your positive choices into habits can take time. You can easily slip into old behaviors and thoughts. You can easily start to feed the bad wolf. It's completely understandable and relatable.

This is why I suggest that you take the time to turn happiness into a habit. And the easiest way to do this is by setting aside time to journal every single day. Throughout this book, I have suggested several journaling activities, but I want to focus on the importance of journaling as a habit. The act of taking pen to paper makes a thought real. It turns an abstraction into something tangible. By journaling, you commit. You give your thoughts power when you put them down on paper.

By simply taking note of something positive every day, you reinforce your commitment to feeding the good wolf. By letting your thoughts flow freely through your pen, you can see them clearly and can identify disruptive thoughts that are entering your head. When you are aware of disruptive thoughts, you have a chance to replace them with positive, inspiring thoughts. Journaling gives you this chance.

CRAFT A LIFE YOU LOVE

It has been said that it takes twenty-one days to form a new habit, so here are twenty-one prompts that you can use to begin making happiness a habit through the power of journaling. Set aside five, ten, or fifteen minutes at the same time each day and answer a prompt.

The process should feel freeing. Write down the first thing that comes to your mind. Don't overthink it or judge your words or thoughts. Remember that your goal is to make happiness a habit, so do your best to write down positive thoughts.

1. I feel childlike joy when...

_____

_____

_____

_____

_____

2. Who is someone that gives me tremendous energy and why?

_____

_____

_____

_____

_____

_____

3. What are some values that I love in a person? Why do I love these values?

_____

_____

_____

_____

_____

4. The best thing that happened yesterday was...

_____

_____

_____

_____

_____

5. What is a risk that I am excited to take?

_____

_____

_____

_____

_____

6. One of my favorite memories is...

_____

_____

_____

_____

7. If I were going to have a dance party and behave like
a fool, who are the people I would invite and why? What
songs would we listen to?

_____

_____

_____

_____

8. I feel special when...

_____

_____

_____

_____

9. What are some things I can do to make sure that I feel
happy each and every day?

_____

_____

_____

_____

_____

10. What do I stand for?

_____

_____

_____

_____

11. What is something that made me laugh really hard recently?

_____

_____

_____

_____

12. I can tell that the Universe is looking out for me because...

_____

_____

_____

_____

13. Today I am thankful for...

_____

_____

_____

_____

14. What does a perfect day look like?

_____

_____

_____

_____

15. What are five things I believe in with all of my heart?

_____

_____

_____

_____

16. What is something uncommon and wonderful that surprises people about me?

_____

_____

_____

_____

17. Something wonderful is starting to bloom inside of me. It is...

_____

_____

_____

_____

18. What is something I would like to do to make this world a better place?

_____

_____

_____

_____

19. It is important that _____ feels loved by me. What is something I can do to make sure of that?

_____

_____

_____

_____

20. What is the word that I love the most, and why?

_____

_____

_____

_____

21. If I could talk to one person today and say one thing, who would it be and why?

_____

_____

_____

_____

jack's bedtime ritual

—

'll confess that, before Jack was born, I did not entirely understand the importance of bedtime rituals. It was a mystery to me why my friends with children had to leave dinner a little early just to make sure they didn't interrupt their young children's bedtime rituals. I found my critical internal voice wondering, *Is fifteen minutes really that big of a deal? Just throw some pajamas on them and stick them in bed.*

I am officially eating crow.

Now that I have a child, I understand. If Jack's bedtime routine doesn't start by 7:30 P.M., everything falls apart. He gets overly tired during his bath, which ends up winding him up, and then we have to spend an extra thirty minutes negotiating how many books we are going to read. Then, the next day he either has to sleep in—which means his nap is later, which means bedtime is later—or we wake him at his usual time and he is fussy throughout the day. We must deal with random tantrums about major decisions, such as throwing away wrappers versus keeping them.

Honoring the bedtime ritual is a matter of life and death. (Well, not really, but you get the point.)

The word *ritual* might sound extreme, but rituals actually give the brain and your emotions cues about what you should be doing and how you should be feeling. If you create rituals surrounding your craft, you will have an easier time engaging in doing what you love, and you will be more committed to making a habit out of pursuing your craft.

Here are some examples of rituals:

- Going to a favorite coffee shop before writing
- Turning on your favorite music, steeping some tea, and sitting in your favorite chair before knitting
- Taking a walk in nature before returning to your home studio to paint
- Closing the door, silencing your cell phone, and picking up your favorite colored pencils before sketching

All of these rituals send your mind and your body cues that it is time for you to begin practicing your craft. And I argue that these rituals are critically important. Without them, your practice could be hit or miss. Just like Jack's bedtime and the day after can be disrupted if we do not honor his bedtime ritual, your craft could be interrupted if you do not prepare your mind and your body to fully enter your creative zone.

CRAFT A LIFE YOU LOVE

You may have only ten minutes to work on your craft, but I suggest spending a few moments to settle in before you begin. Honor your craft with a ritual. Allow it to flourish and flow.

What ritual can you build around your craft?

_____

_____

_____

when no one else is awake

—

Here is something surprising: When your brain is fatigued, it has a harder time remembering the existing connections that it has formed between ideas and concepts. This means that you might actually be more creative when your brain is fuzzy. (This might be why so many creative types are night owls. They thrive and function better after dark, when they can find more peace and solitude.) This runs contrary to popular sentiment, which says that you will do your best work when your brain is freshest and the most alert. But when your brain is fatigued, it might make unusual and creative connections. It might be open to new ideas. It might reveal things that your alert, focused mind would not see.

This is why I like to work in the early morning. I have discovered that I am most creative when I first wake up, when I am groggy. Plus, when I wake up before Jack, before JC, and before my phone starts buzzing, I can sit with myself and my ideas, giving them the full attention they deserve.

So it should come as no surprise that I recommend that you make a habit of investing time in your hobby as your first to-do item when you wake up, even if it is just a few minutes. And by this, I mean *before you check your email, before you look at Instagram or Twitter, and even before you drink a cup of coffee!* (However, if your creative ritual includes having the cup of coffee, do what works!)

By investing time in your hobby as soon as you wake up, your mind will be clear from the night's thoughts, and you will be open to new connections. In the early morning light, you will see your hobby in a new way, making creative connections and solving problems that seemed difficult to solve the day before. In a perfect world, you could wake up and actually engage in your hobby for as long as you would like. And if your day allows you to do this, by all means, go for it! Imagine how great you will feel if you start your day off by doing something you love!

However, starting your day off by fully engaging in your craft is probably unrealistic on most days. You may have lunches to make, school to attend, work meetings scheduled, and business trips to take. You likely don't have thirty or sixty minutes to spend on your craft, but you probably *do* have two or three minutes.

When I only have a few minutes to focus, here's what I do:

1. I free-form—write, draw, or sketch. Sometimes I write about last night's dream, sometimes I draw, sometimes I do both. I never edit or worry about whether my writing makes sense. I just stay open to whatever comes to me. And I do this every day, without fail. By writing down my thoughts, I find that my strongest desires have a place to manifest themselves repeatedly. Writing this book was a goal I've had for many years. It kept showing up during these free-form sessions, which meant that it was important and should be pursued.

2. Then I make myself two promises:
I promise that I will make a specific healthy choice that day. It might be a physical choice, such as "I am going to run two miles after this," or something for my mental health, such as "I won't let things that are out of my control bother me. I will do the best that I can."

Then, **I promise to write down my top priority for the day.** I think of it like this: If I get nothing else accomplished, what is the one thing that has to happen in order for me to feel as if my day has been successful? In this way, I declare to myself that I am here to create and to make my life happen. I also remind myself that I am in charge of my day.

Thrive in a creative ritual of your choice.

(MORNING OR NIGHT? IT'S UP TO YOU.)

CRAFT A LIFE YOU LOVE

By now, you know that I am a huge fan of writing things down. Why not start your morning by spending a few minutes describing what you are going to do that day to move your craft forward? Perhaps this is a simple to-do list. Perhaps it is a description of an idea that you have. Whatever it is, put your idea on paper first thing in the morning. Then, revisit it when the time is right.

looking somewhere else

—

Anyone who has ever found something that he or she thought was forever lost will appreciate this.

While looking for one of Jack's little blue socks, I stumbled upon a lost lens cap. When I found it, I let out a little shriek of joy that surprised Jack. It even surprised me.

I had invested hours—dare I say days—looking for this cap. Finding it had been an irrational obsession: me against the house elves who steal things like lens caps, socks (one at a time), and car keys. (Do the elves do this to drive us crazy, to keep us off balance, or to keep us humble?) After days of fruitless searching for the lens cap, I had begrudgingly made peace with the probability that I would never see it again.

And just like that, while looking for that little blue sock, the lens cap came back to me! Hallelujah! All was right in the world again.

It got me thinking that perhaps the elves stole that cap to give me the gift of insight. I had looked in all the conventional places I had expected to find a lens cap, but it was somewhere else. Sometimes the answer is not where you expect to find it.

As artists (and yes, you are an artist), we draw inspiration from all sorts of places. We often find things, solve problems, or gain insight from unexpected sources. Sometimes, our best creations or our best solutions require us to find perspective from somewhere outside of conventional thinking. We must search where we would not think to look to find our answer.

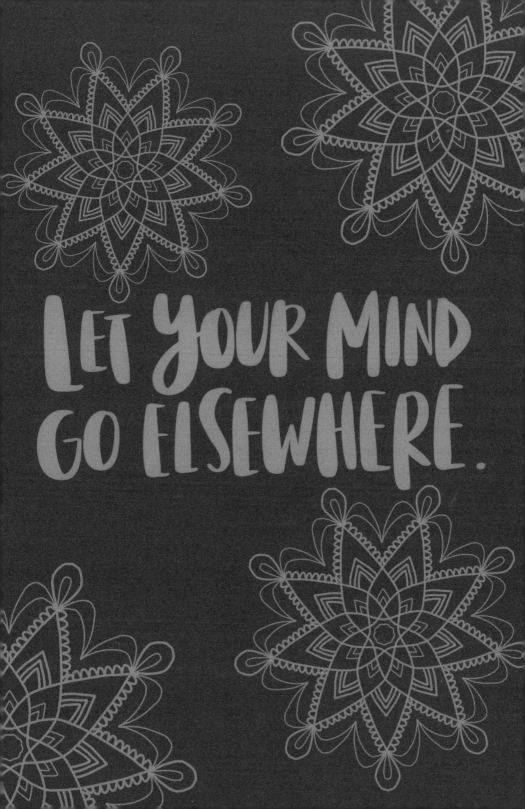

So, while it might sound counterintuitive, if you want to improve your craft, here is my advice: Spend time elsewhere. Let your mind go somewhere else. Let your craft gestate quietly in the background. Trust that the inspiration can and will show up in unexpected ways.

> **Every individual has the ability to create ideas based on his or her existing patterns of thinking. These patterns follow a route ingrained in our youth as we were being taught to think. But without any provision for variations, ideas eventually stagnate and lose their adaptive advantages.**
> —MICHELLE MICHALKO

Artists know that looking at the same sources for inspiration over and over again will actually cause creativity to stagnate. One of the most critical aspects of being an artist is the ability to draw new connections and to find inspiration in new places.

I practice what Raphael DiLuzio and other creativity experts call "divergent thinking." For me, one of the most effective activities to promote divergent thinking is to start a side project: I create work completely unrelated to my core project.

With my mind fully occupied with something else, new perspectives and ideas begin to emerge unexpectedly. Just like looking for the little blue sock revealed my lost lens cap, with ease I discover a fresh approach, or even a novel full-blown idea. When I put myself in new situations, I solve problems, discover ways of growing, and learn things about myself that I never knew.

For instance, a dear friend and I had a falling out. I made an error in judgment on a night when I definitely overindulged in the alcohol department. We had a misunderstanding, and I felt terrible because she felt hurt. I was partially at fault, so I admitted my blunder and apologized. She may have overreacted a bit but didn't admit this at first. I found myself ruminating on the situation, focusing on the fact that I had apologized profusely, whereas she seemed unwilling to give in. We were unable to resolve our differences; it felt as if we were running in circles. We decided we needed to take a little break to get some perspective.

Several weeks later, when I was reading a book, the answer came to me. I finally understood her outlook. I realized that she was unable to accept my apology because I had apologized for the wrong thing. With one simple conversation, I was able to acknowledge my wrongdoing, explain that I was attempting to correct course, and she and I were able to find common ground again.

CRAFT A LIFE YOU LOVE

Inspiration comes from many places, so put yourself in
new situations as often as possible. Make a list of things
unrelated to your craft that might enrich your life.

New books to read:

_____

_____

_____

New movies to see:

_____

_____

_____

Projects to work on:

_____

_____

_____

_____

Classes to take:

_____

_____

_____

_____

People to get to know better:

_____

_____

_____

Places to visit:

_____

_____

_____

_____

This week, try something new:

Spend time with a person you have been wanting
to know better.

If you always read fiction, read a biography.

If you never watch the History Channel, turn it
on this week.

If you are feeling really bold, sign up for
a class that makes you feel a little bit nervous.

Knowing what inspires you to live your best creative
life is key. Often the best way to learn is to just
take the first step and start going through a new process.
You don't need to have all the answers and resources
right away, you just need to believe and begin. Evolve,
grow, and try new things.

detox

——

What would happen if you stayed away from technology for forty-eight hours? What would you do differently? How much time would you spend on your craft or on other hobbies?

I went on a forty-eight-hour screen detox. It started on a Friday afternoon when Jack, JC, and I were on vacation. I felt excitement, but also a bit of fear. I run a business, so I was not entirely prepared for a complete detox. I cheated a bit: I gave myself thirty minutes of screen time and allowed myself to use my camera because I wanted to document our trip.

Here is what happened:

1. I learned to live in the moment.

The first night was a breeze. We spent time with friends we see only once a year. Being able to really be present and enjoy everyone's company was wonderful. As the archivist, I was called upon to take a group photo before it got dark. It took more time getting the twenty-five of us situated than it did to wirelessly send the photo from my camera to my phone to be shared via AirDrop. That was five minutes of my grace period well spent, because the moment captured will be treasured for years to come. That evening, I played Catch Phrase until I wore myself out.

After I got into bed, I still felt the need to do something, so I took the opportunity to dive into a book instead of picking up my phone. I can assure you that I would not have gotten through half a book in forty-eight hours if a screen had been available.

2. I took it all in.

We spent Saturday at the beach, enjoying our last day of vacation. As we sat under the umbrella, it was relaxing to take in my surroundings. The urge to Snapchat those moments came on strong, but I resisted. The feeling passed, and I simply tried to focus on being completely present.

In the evening, we enjoyed a lovely dinner, and Jack discovered the joy of dominoes. Without a distraction, I was able to fully relish the anticipation that came over him as his grandfather set the up entire box in a snake pattern on the coffee table.

3. I discovered a new way to travel.

On Sunday, we headed back home at 4:00 A.M. My rule on the plane for my toddler is that there are no rules. If he wants to watch TV the entire time, he can watch TV. If he wants to eat lollipops instead of lunch, that is cool, too. He was taking his forty-fifth and forty-sixth flights, and I wasn't about to change our streak of smooth airplane rides.

I, however, had a slightly difficult time without watching a movie or playing a game on my phone. Instead, I found refuge in reading, journaling, and watercoloring in my traveler's notebook. My reflections and thoughts are now documented on the pages of the book along with photos, providing evidence of our good times.

Jack wanted to cuddle, and he fell asleep in my arms. I spied JC in the row in front of us watching golf, and I felt a twinge of jealousy. I had to work hard to resist the urge to pull out my phone.

For nearly two hours, I couldn't do much of anything. I knew Jack needed the sleep, so I decided to sit with my thoughts. I ended up having a couple of sentimental hours thinking about motherhood, Jack, and JC. As I watched my beautiful child sleep, I reflected on my blessings and the love I have for my life. Those were probably the best two hours of the trip.

Though it wasn't easy to spend that time without technology, it gave me time to reflect, appreciate, and discover what can happen when I am "doing nothing." It was worth it, and my new goal is to take time daily to unplug and really be present in a way that doesn't involve a screen.

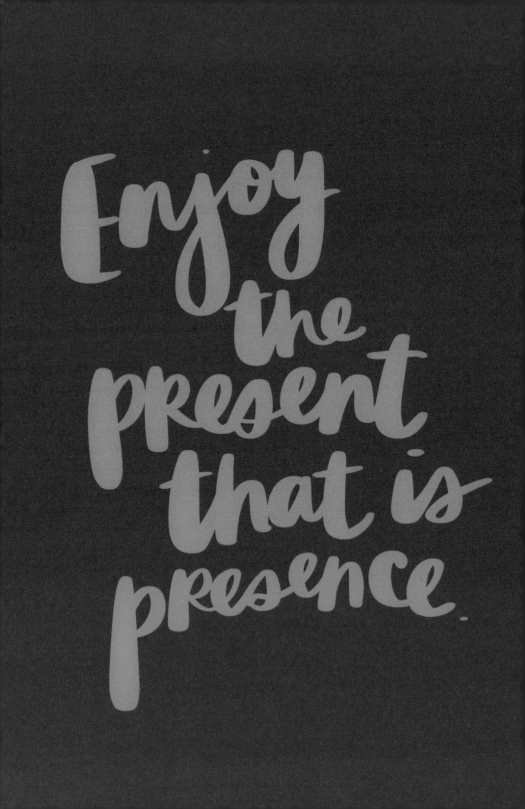

CRAFT A LIFE YOU LOVE

You know what is coming, right? Your assignment is to make a habit out of screen detoxing. Your detox does not have to be forty-eight hours, but it should happen regularly enough that it becomes a habit. I want you to get comfortable living without a screen during certain times. Perhaps it is for two hours once a week, or just during meals. Whatever it is, be sure to document whatever unfolds for you when you give up the screen.

What did I experience that I would not have experienced if I had been in front of a screen?

_____

_____

_____

_____

_____

What little observations did I make that I may have overlooked if I had been distracted?

_____

_____

_____

_____

_____

PART FIVE

—

crafting your
WAY BACK

on losing your creative mojo

—

When I was thirty years old, I took a little sabbatical from my career. Today, I call it my one-third-life crisis. I was overworked and burnt out, and I felt lost. I had also recently ended a relationship with my long-term boyfriend. He worked with me and we had raised two dogs together, so our lives were quite intertwined. At the time, I felt like my twenties were so eventful and fun. I felt successful on my own terms. I believed that everything was going to tumble downhill after thirty.

Of course, I now know that isn't true. During the crisis I focused on self-care and found increased vitality. I followed my intuition and worked hard to perfect "the art of truly living." This was a concept I learned about from a workshop with the amazing artist Sabrina Ward Harrison. It was a time when my head was in the clouds, but I had one foot on the ground. I reconnected with friends from college. I met and fell in love with JC. A few years later, I had Jack. Now I feel more fulfillment and happiness in my career than ever before. My thirties have been wonderful!

We all have crises—quarter-life crises, midlife crises, and just plain ol' crises. We lose relationships, jobs, goals. We lose a sense of self. And among the saddest of all, we can lose our creative mojo.

Among the saddest of all? you might be thinking.

Yes. I stand by my position that your creative side projects are among the most important aspects of your happiness. These hobbies represent your soul expressing itself. When you knit a hat for an unborn baby, you express the love you already feel for that child and his or her parents. When you make the place cards for your Thanksgiving dinner by hand, you tell the people in your home that they are welcome, loved, and worthy of your time. When you carefully tend your flower garden, you nurture the potential for beauty in the world.

I have noticed in my own life that my desire to create is diminished during the times when I feel my worst. I have also noticed that these are the times when creation is the most important. Focusing on the growth mindset is vital when you are feeling down. It's okay to pause and rest, but also to focus your energies on experiences that make you thrive.

I deepened my connection with the scrapbooking community during my one-third-life crisis. I saw two of the Seven Wonders of the World (traveling is a big hobby of mine). I took surfing and snowboarding lessons. I turned to inspiring quotes to help me raise myself up. And my first scrapbook page was published in a national magazine.

I have never walked away from a creation without feeling a sense of peace—if only for a few moments. I now know that during times of sadness, creation is my relief. Perhaps you feel the same way. Crafting allows us to form a deeper connection to ourselves, which means we get closer to our sense of purpose.

Creation is often the path to healing. In the moments when you lose yourself in the flow of your creation, you actually find your true self again. Through the process, you spend time reflecting. You reconnect with familiar positive feelings and remember who you are, why you are unique and important, and what you most value. We are all works in progress. Lifting one another up contributes greatly to the whole of the creative community. The collective consciousness of positivity and strength has tremendous power and effect. You never know who or what you'll inspire. Share your gifts.

When you just don't *feel* like creating, what can you do? What is the path back? When I'm stuck in my head about losing my creative mojo, I identify a worthy recipient.

It will be easier for you to find a path out of sadness or defeat if you focus on another person. Ruminating on your own unhappiness can keep you stuck in the moment of unhappiness. One feeling of emptiness leads to more and more feelings of emptiness. It is a vicious cycle. But if you think about the people you love—the people who inspire you—then it becomes easier to move beyond your own feelings of inadequacy or disappointment and focus on something (or, in this case, someone) that makes you feel happy.

Just as ruminating on unhappy feelings can perpetuate cycles of unhappiness, focusing on a feeling of happiness can produce more feelings of happiness. My friend Jennifer helps organize these amazing card drives. The purpose is to collect cards for those in need of a little cheering up. Card-makers from around the world participate in creating beautiful handmade cards. They send them to Jennifer, who then passes them along to worthy recipients. Sometimes the cards are for elderly people who live in nursing homes and may feel lonely or isolated. Other times, they go to members of the military who are not able to go shopping for a card to send home to their families.

My point is that together we can inspire one another and lift each other up. I, for one, feel incredibly lucky and blessed to be doing what I love for a living and to be sharing it with all of you. I have days when I am not "feeling it," and I think it would be easier to get a steady job with a regular paycheck. Then I receive little reminders from friends that we, as a creative community, are all in this together, and we need to support one another.

Share your gifts. We are all a work in progress. We can all do good things and make a positive impact in our communities and in the world. You never know who or what you will inspire, but one thing is certain— when you share your gift, you *will* inspire yourself.

CRAFT A LIFE YOU LOVE

Identify a worthy recipient to share your creative gifts with this week. You could create something for a friend who has been particularly supportive, a relative going through a tough time, or a child whose innocence is refreshing. Turning your thoughts toward this person can inspire you to create. You might not feel like doing it for yourself, but you can probably get excited about doing it for someone else.

And with one creation down, who knows? You might just feel like embarking on another creation.

Who is a worthy recipient of your craft today?

_____

_____

_____

_____

_____

_____

_____

_____

_____

_____

easy does it

—

My dad is an engineer, so he was thrilled when I was accepted to the Georgia Institute of Technology, or, as it is more commonly known, Georgia Tech. Being admitted felt good, but actually attending Georgia Tech did not. While I had a lot of fun outside of class and made some lifelong friends, the actual school part of it was difficult. I spent two years at Georgia Tech studying industrial design, which meant that I spent a lot of time in the studio working for hours on end on various projects. From my first day there, I felt overwhelmed. I was studying so hard that it did not seem as if I had time for anything else. The real bummer was that, even though I was putting in a ton of effort, I was bringing home Bs and Cs. Other people around me—people who didn't seem to be working as hard as I was—were making more progress and getting better grades than I was.

I knew why. I could see it on their faces: They loved industrial design. It was their passion.

My passion, however, was making and designing clothes. Even though I enjoyed the aesthetics of industrial design, I was not good at it. And not being good at something I spent so much time and effort on did not make me come alive. Unfortunately, Georgia Tech does not offer a degree in fashion design, so after struggling academically for two and a half years, I asked my dad (who was paying my tuition) if I could transfer to American Intercontinental University. While AIU was not as well-known, it was the only college in Atlanta at the time offering a degree in fashion design and marketing.

It wasn't a conventional move. A lot of people would probably love to hang a degree from Georgia Tech on their wall. And, to be honest, the decision was hard. I knew I was just two years away from having a degree that I could leverage for the rest of my life. Still, I decided to walk away.

Pursuing a degree in fashion design felt a lot easier. At Georgia Tech, I felt as if I never had time for anything but school; when I enrolled at AIU, I suddenly felt as if I had a lot more time to pursue other opportunities. I took a part-time job at a restaurant and interned at a modeling agency answering phones.

One day, a photographer I met at the modeling agency asked me if I had ever considered being a fashion stylist. I knew very little about styling, but I was certainly interested! He and I had a meeting, and we decided to put together a shoot. The manager of the restaurant I worked at agreed to let us use it as a location. We booked models through Elite Model Management, and I bought a bunch of dresses (which I returned the day after the shoot). We also had an awesome hair and makeup artist.

I styled and produced the shoot. It felt so good having creatives come together to make this happen. Though we were not getting paid, everyone was putting his or her time and resources in so we could have the shot for our portfolios. When we saw the results, we were all so happy.

Immediately, Elite Model Management called and signed me on as one of their fashion stylists. It was a big break. During my first two and a half years of college, I had felt frustrated and overwhelmed. During my last two years, I felt energized.

I enjoyed every moment. I had some challenging times, of course, but it felt as if I was starting to build something meaningful and fun. Collaborating with like-minded creative people felt freeing and full of possibility. Looking back, I had found my tribe, and discovered the true meaning of collaboration.

In retrospect, I think I probably worked just as hard at AIU as I did at Georgia Tech, but because I wasn't depleted, I felt as if I had more energy to pursue other side projects: I had time to be a freelance fashion stylist, work at a modeling agency, and make extra money as a restaurant hostess.

I could have stuck it out at Georgia Tech, and I would have received a more prestigious degree. But I likely would have felt drained and would have taken a different career path—and I never would have had that big break as a fashion stylist.

Here is the lesson I learned, and the reason I am telling you this story: Sometimes, the best choice is just to keep things simple. People think that *simple* sounds pedestrian, but I don't think it is. To me, *simple* means "essential." It means focusing on priorities and nothing else. It means extracting yourself from things that are extraneous.

If something feels overly complex, it is probably going to spill into other areas of your life, taking resources away from things that are important to you. In this way, *simple* isn't pedestrian at all—it is an evolved way of living!

CRAFT A LIFE YOU LOVE

When you are feeling overwhelmed, or when you feel
frustrated and dissatisfied, start creating something
that you know will feel simple. Think about your go-to
projects, the ones that you can do in your sleep. Sew
a little gift tag, or paint a background for a scrapbook
page using your favorite supplies. Bake some cookies.
Crochet a little baby hat. As your mind and your body
relax, you will start to see everything clearly.
Everything will come into focus, you will be able to
pick out the things that need your attention, and you
will find ways to eliminate the excess.

thinking inside the box

—

Much attention is placed on the importance of thinking *outside* the box, but, to be frank, nothing seems more intimidating to me than thinking outside the box. Think of it like this: Imagine that you call and ask me to design a dress for you. I ask you what you envision, and you say, "I don't know. I just want you to design a dress for me."

Where am I to begin? I have the full rainbow of colors to choose from, as well as every fabric and pattern imaginable. Should I design a dress for a casual weekend get-together or a formal wedding? Should the dress be formfitting or free-flowing?

Now imagine that you call me and say, "I want a sleeveless, bright aqua blue dress with a choker collar, and a fit that hugs my waist and flares at my knees like a mermaid's tail in a size six."

Now I can get started!

"The more constraints one imposes, the more one frees one's self . . . the arbitrariness of the constraint serves only to obtain precision of execution."

—IGOR STRAVINSKY

I find that I am most creative when I have boundaries to work against or parameters to work within. When I am struggling with a creative problem or with creative output in general, I often create artificial constraints as a way to find a new solution or to get forward momentum.

For instance, when I know I have a deadline to meet for a client's scrapbook, I start by pulling together a small kit in one style, with matching colors and embellishments. Instead of taking out all of my supplies and choosing from dozens of colors and styles and hundreds of embellishments, I start with the photos and memorabilia and add accents from the kit. This streamlines decisions and allows me to focus on the key elements. Sometimes I give myself a constraint of time. I decide that whatever time limit I set will be enough time. I can very often crank out even more than I thought.

My point is this: The constraint, whatever it is, supports action.

Imagine that I ask you to write a poem and read it in front of a room full of people. Unless you are a poet, I suspect this causes you to break into a cold sweat. But what if instead I gave you a newspaper clipping and said, "Write a fifteen-word poem that tells the story of your soul using words that you find in this article."

I bet you could do it, right? I bet you would also have fun doing it.

CRAFT A LIFE YOU LOVE

Poet Austin Kleon has made a name for himself by using the constraints of an existing page of a newspaper. He blacks out all but a few words, and his poem emerges from the structure provided by another writer. He calls this process "creation through subtraction."

Give his exercise a try. Pull a page out of a book, newspaper, or magazine and paste it onto the next page. Select fifteen words from that page to write your own personal manifesto.

Manifesto

_____

_____

_____

_____

_____

_____

_____

_____

_____

_____

_____

Paste your page here.

lost . . . in the right place

———

Shortly after I lost out on money due to my inability to deliver all of the T-shirts ordered during the trade show (see page 89), I decided to enter into an agreement with another company that had more capacity than I did. This company handled all the production and day-to-day work, which freed me up to focus on design and styling for my line, Amy Tangerine, as well as one of the larger company's lines. For the first time in my life, at twenty-three years of age, I had a decent, steady paycheck, and things seemed to be going smoothly for me.

Because I was responsible for styling an umbrella company's catalog, as well as consulting on design and marketing for its collection, I was traveling back and forth between Atlanta and Los Angeles frequently. Five months into our relationship, the owner of the larger company asked if I would consider relocating to Los Angeles to take a more active position within the company. It seemed like an amazing opportunity that I could not pass up. I rented my condo to a friend, gave my car to my mom in Chicago, and packed everything else into a moving truck. My belongings would arrive in Los Angeles about three weeks later, giving me more than enough time to find a place in Santa Monica as close to the beach as I could afford.

The timing of the move was great. I had a trade show in Los Angeles that I needed to attend anyway, so I bought my one-way ticket. When I arrived in Los Angeles, I checked into a downtown hotel with three suit-cases. My plan was to stay in the hotel, then with friends, buy a car, look for a place to live, and get settled into my new life on the West Coast.

I wrote a check for a silver Volkswagen Beetle convertible on my second Friday morning in Los Angeles, and I planned to spend the weekend apartment hunting. I had stayed at a friend's house in Venice during the week and checked into the Viceroy Hotel in Santa Monica with my friend Lauren after work. Right before Lauren and I were walking out of the hotel room to get dinner, I got a phone call that pivoted my life in a way that was most unexpected. My boss told me that I was going to be let go if I chose to keep Amy Tangerine on the side. I had to choose: either the company I created, or the job that had moved me to Los Angeles.

This was no small problem. My mom had been laid off from her job with the airlines in the summer of 2003. She was doing a lot of the work for Amy Tangerine from Chicago. For that reason alone, I was not going to give up Amy Tangerine. But even if my mom had not been working for me, I would not have walked away from my line. I told my boss as much, and I was let go.

I was living in a hotel, which meant I was paying four times the amount I would have paid in rent. My furniture was somewhere in the middle of America, and I had just purchased a brand-new car. I was shocked. And in tears. I had no idea what to do next.

I was lost, so I immediately called my parents. My dad said something that stuck with me: He said that I was lost in the right place.

Those words comforted me. They made me grateful that my parents had instilled in me the value of saving money. I had no idea what my next move was going to be, but I knew this: I would not have moved to Los Angeles on my own. I needed to have a reason to move across the country. That job—the very one I was being let go from—brought me to Los Angeles. And I knew my future was here. I was where I needed to be for a reason. I needed to see what would happen next, and I needed to be open to the possibility that, even though I was lost, I was still in the right place.

I did not know what I had to do, but I knew I had to do something. As is always the case during transitions, I turned to my craft. I started networking and freelancing, and soon thereafter, I was hired by Hudson Jeans to design a T-shirt line. It was a huge breakthrough for me. Through Hudson

Jeans, I met a person who had embroidery machines that could replicate the T-shirts that we had been stitching by hand. (Collaborating with people who understand your creative vision and can execute it is huge!)

Eventually, my freelancing gigs opened up doors to contractors and resources that were plentiful in Los Angeles. I never would have been given these opportunities if I had stayed in Atlanta. I decided to take a huge leap of faith and focus on my company full-time.

Our paths do not always turn out how we envision them. Often, there are twists and turns that we are not able to predict. Yet, when we find ourselves in pivotal moments where we feel uncertain, these are the times when it is absolutely essential to dig deeper to seek meaning and uncover essential truths.

One of the lessons I learned during this period was that because my problem was big, I had to find a big solution. That's the great thing about big problems: You cannot ignore them. You have to make adjustments. They force you to focus on your strengths and the things that are in your control. In fact, in some ways, smaller problems can be a bigger threat because they can be left unattended. But when you find yourself completely lost with a huge problem, then you have no choice: You are in the right place to find a huge solution.

CRAFT A LIFE YOU LOVE

When we feel lost, we panic, and our brains tend to
shut down. Eventually, our brains begin to regulate,
and we are able to find realistic solutions. The feeling
of being overwhelmed diminishes and our thoughts shift
to solutions intuitively. Our purpose becomes clearer
and more focused.

Here are some journaling prompts that can take you
from a big problem to a big solution:

This feels like an impossible problem to solve.
MacGyver might be able to solve it, but no one else
could. Make a list of all the things you are feeling.
It is okay to be overwhelmed.

_____

_____

_____

_____

What is the worst-case scenario? (These things we
make up in our heads almost never happen.)

_____

_____

_____

_____

_____

_____

If you were to ask a five-year-old to solve this problem
for you, what would the five-year-old suggest?

_____

_____

_____

_____

_____

Okay, what are ten tiny things that you can do to take a
small step toward solving this problem?

1. _____

_____

2. _____

_____

3. _____

_____

4. _____

_____

5. _____

_____

6. _____

_____

7. _____

_____

8. _____

_____

9. _____

_____

10. _____

_____

Which one of these ten things can you do today?

_____

_____

_____

_____

_____

_____

_____

_____

on waiting it out

—

n an earlier chapter (see page 28), I wrote about how my dad and I moved from Chicago to Atlanta when I was fifteen. The plan was for my mom to join us the following year, but she never came.

At the time, my mom had been working for the same company in Chicago for nineteen years. At twenty years, she would be eligible for a full pension, so when my dad was offered a job in Atlanta, it made sense for my mom to stay put for one more year so she could quit with full benefits.

Her plan was to wait it out. But six months into the plan, my mom was laid off.

This came as a pretty big blow. The upside was that she could move to Atlanta sooner than expected, which was what my dad and I assumed would happen. But she didn't move. She was depressed, and she wanted to be close to her parents and brothers, all of whom lived in Chicago. After this unexpected life change, moving to a new state felt too overwhelming, so instead, she got a job at a friend's restaurant as a manager.

She promised she would move to Atlanta, but she explained that she needed some time before she could handle yet another adjustment. Again, her plan was to wait it out.

And then came the biggest blow of all: My mom's dad died. I can only imagine how devastated my mom was—aside from my parents, he was my favorite person in the world. After his passing, Chicago became even more important to her: Her family members in Chicago were the only connection she had left to her dad. Again, her plan was to wait it out. She would come to Atlanta when her grief passed.

Meanwhile, my dad was in Atlanta living with a boy-crazy teenaged daughter. He felt lonely, and he wanted his wife by his side. The longer it took for my mom to arrive, the more he believed she would never come. Eventually, he filed for divorce.

I cannot say that this was true at the time, but today, I do not hold any resentment toward either of my parents. I know they have always wanted the best for me, and they have repeatedly proven this to me.

Today my mom lives in our guesthouse in Los Angeles, and she has more than made up for any lost time. She was a huge part of my T-shirt business and is probably my biggest cheerleader. She helps with Jack and she cooks, cleans, and runs errands. My dad is remarried and still plays tennis. He lives north of Atlanta and is *almost* retired. He loves his work and his grandson. We try to see him and his wife, Julia, several times a year. I'm so grateful they enjoy traveling and make the trip to see us in Los Angeles as much as they can.

I did learn a big lesson from the period before my parents' divorce: Waiting things out is rarely the answer. Life is happening today. More important than the future are the seconds and the minutes of your life *today*. How are you spending them? Are you spending them with love, being certain that each one is honored and nurtured? Or are you throwing them away, being frivolous with them, allowing yourself to sink into a funk?

On quite a few occasions, I have been tempted to wait things out— relationships, goals, conversations. But adding time to the equation usually only amplifies the problem. Not only am I losing precious time, but I am also creating a situation that requires a lot more effort than would be necessary if I had just done something when I knew something needed to be done.

Plus, we waste so much energy when we postpone taking action. How must my mom have felt each time she heard the phone ring, knowing that my dad might be on the other end of the line, feeling sad and confused?

How must she have felt at night, knowing that she had a decision to make, but not knowing when or how to make the decision?

Every day we are given the opportunity to do things, to make things, and to make things happen. Talking about dreams is great, but taking small steps toward achieving them is way better. Allow your ideas to come to fruition and don't wait on important things. As a natural procrastinator, I have to consistently work on this. A wise mentor told me something that has stuck with me: "It's not how many ideas you have, it's how many you make happen."

CRAFT A LIFE YOU LOVE

When you take care of the things you have to take care of—the relationships, the goals, and the conversations—you make room for the next thing to happen, and the next thing to happen. It creates positive momentum that allows for more movement, progress, and potential breakthroughs.

And this is the way life goes: The next thing *is* going to happen, and it's either going to be something that you manifest and create, or it is going to be something that someone else creates. Remember, you create your own happiness.

Make a bucket list of the big things you want to accomplish one day in your journal. Here is an example from my bucket list:

Write a book (YAY! You're holding it!)

Travel to every continent

Go skydiving

Pay for my kid's college tuition

Donate more each and every year

Now, write down the tiny steps you can take today toward crossing off one of the things on your bucket list.

Bucket List

_____

_____

_____

_____

_____

_____

_____

_____

_____

_____

_____

_____

_____

_____

_____

crafting your
PASSIONS

no doubt

—

n today's world, one only needs to look around to find tons of seemingly self-assured people who have found success by pursuing their creative passions. Turn on the television to see A-list actors being interviewed about the highly rated films they've been working on. Walk through your local museum to find thousands of years' worth of incredible art. Scroll through Instagram and you'll find models and photographers with hundreds of thousands of followers making life seem so glamorous while sipping on beautiful lattes in their latest photos. Take a minute to pull up YouTube's homepage and their algorithm will suggest viral videos created by seemingly instant superstars with millions of subscribers.

We rarely see the mother who stitches sweet embroidery pieces while her kids nap, the aspiring author trying to find a publisher, or the teenager putting herself through college who makes hand-painted cards for birthdays because she can't afford to buy them in stores. These people aren't in the spotlight, but they are all around us every day and their passions are just as valid as anyone else's—as are yours!

Thanks to the Internet, it can sometimes feel overwhelming to jump headfirst into trying something new. The online world offers easy access to artists and makers who have already gone through the process of discovering what they're passionate about, so we forget how much work, waiting, heartbreak, and starting over had to happen to get them there. For that reason, it's so easy to stop trying when we don't find immediate success. Sadly, it's even more common to not try at all.

Nearly everyone can name something they are drawn to like a magnet, but there are a few more steps to take if you want to go from someone who appreciates a medium to someone who creates within that medium. When you're admiring beautifully hand-lettered journals or incredibly detailed paintings, it can be so easy to shrug it off as something you could never do.

My friend and fellow YouTube creator Lauren Fairweather said this: "Whenever I post tutorial videos teaching how to make the craft projects I design, I receive comments from viewers saying that they love the project but they would never be able to make it themselves. I try my hardest to encourage them to give it a try because they were clearly drawn to the craft in the first place. Unfortunately, no matter how hard I work to provide clear instructions and a positive environment for creating, sometimes their self-doubt is just too much of an obstacle."

As someone who works to teach and inspire others to be creative, I often hear things to that effect. When I was in Brazil teaching workshops, a very talented woman who seemed quiet and shy asked the translator to tell me what an inspiration I was and how my designs were her favorites. Before long, I could tell she understood what I was saying and that her English was actually very good. When I told her this, she responded, "But I have a doubt." I immediately understood that although she was confident in her ability to create, she was reluctant to express herself using a language she didn't think she was good at speaking. When I reassured her that I could understand everything she was saying and she could just try talking to me directly, she gave me a huge hug. From that moment on, she seemed confident not only on paper, but also in talking about her creations! So, you see, the removal of doubt can often expose something that was right there the whole time.

work your way through it

—

People tend to forget that there is a difference between innate talent and hard work. We hear so many stories about childhood prodigies who have always known what they've wanted to do and perform that skill more naturally and flawlessly than any grown adult ever could. But the truth is that very few people actually fit into that category. The vast majority of the creatives you admire reached their level of skill and success with a whole lot of practice.

If you've been trying to find a way to satisfy your creative urges and keep returning to the same places only to lose your confidence, remember that it wouldn't be fair to compare yourself to the people who inspired you to try something new. They've been where you are and they got out of that funk by sticking with it.

I've also encountered a widespread belief that art isn't worth making unless every attempt is something you're proud of. So many people rush into a new hobby only to abandon it when their first tries don't look like the inspiration they found on Pinterest. I'm constantly making mistakes and even leaving them in my YouTube videos instead of editing them out. The learning comes through the trial-and-error process—even from those who seem to always get things right on the first try. Just don't let something you truly love pass you by simply because it isn't turning out quite the way you had hoped.

I'll bring up a situation that is particularly heartbreaking to me, which will tell you a lot about the kind of person I am and how much creativity and self-expression mean to me. When children are young, they make art with endless excitement and enthusiasm. They color to their hearts' content, ask for specific materials, and, when they've finished, they want to display their creations and share them with everyone they know. And you might point and ask, "What did you make?" and they'll tell you confidently that it's a butterfly. It probably won't even actually look like one, but they're so proud of it anyway because they had a great time making it.

You may be wondering what's so heartbreaking about that. Well, one day, that same child will be a bit older and they'll be making something in art class when the cool kid in class points to their project and says something unkind. And eventually, that wonderfully creative child will look at their drawing of a butterfly on the refrigerator and they won't be able to see the butterfly anymore. It'll just look like scribbles. And they'll stop seeing the value in making them.

When you find your butterfly, the one that makes happy flutters in your stomach, the one that you want to share with the world no matter what it looks like, never lose it. Even if it's only something that you bring out when you need a smile and a release from the rest of your stressful day.

coming to the crossroads

—

As adults, we often come to the crossroads of what is practical and what we are truly passionate about. We know we should embrace creative freedom, but the constraints of unfulfilling jobs or too many tasks on our plates at once can hold us back. Adopting a childlike approach takes the pressure off the moment and helps you see your creative path more clearly. An easy way to get into this mindset is to go a whole day pretending you are experiencing everything for the first time. When was the last time you gave your full attention to the colors in a sunset or the taste of a ripe, juicy peach? These simple pleasures are worth revisiting.

"My secret is to try to find delight in everything—from a squirrel running across the yard to the view from my window."

—AMY TANGERINE

Another trick you can try is to turn everyday routines—whether that means working, grocery shopping, or doing chores around the house—into something more enjoyable by mixing things up a bit. If you always start your shopping in a certain part of the store, go the opposite way this week. If you drive the same route to work each day, change it up a bit. You may find new things you like, new places you have never been, and new discoveries in the everyday.

It's so easy to get unhappily stuck in the repetitions of day-to-day living, and we often stay in stuck situations because they keep us in our comfort zones. You might know you're good at something, but continue in a dull job because you're afraid to take the leap and see where you land.

Even when things are going well, we may find ourselves at a crossroads. This is why I find it most important to not only pause and be grateful, but also to keep in mind that change is good (and, frequently, right around the corner). In fact, new passions may be discovered during the times we least expect. One friend of mine discovered her love for photography while she was going through a difficult break-up. When I met JC, he was interviewing for jobs but spending evenings watching *Chopped* and getting creative with his cooking by being frugal in the kitchen. What began as an effort to save money soon bloomed into a true passion.

Although you don't need to wait until you are at a crossroads, the simple acts of adopting a childlike approach, changing everyday routines, and paying attention in times of change allow you to be open in a way that you couldn't be in your regular day, and this openness can lead you to discovering a hobby or passion you'll love doing for the rest of your life.

focus, dream, live

—

As an adult in the digital age, I often find myself reaching for my phone any time I'm in a long line or looking to break away from a mind-numbing task. But there are also plenty of moments when I can't reach Wi-Fi or simply have scrolled through Instagram too many times that day for it to hold my attention any longer. When this happens, I turn to mindfulness. First, I pay attention to the way my body is feeling in that moment. I take a few deep breaths and relax each part of my body, starting from the top of my head and working my way down to the bottoms of my feet. Once I've checked in with my physical state, I then take stock of my surroundings using all of my senses. I notice the warm breeze on my skin. I bask in the beauty of the jacaranda trees in full bloom around my neighborhood. I hear Jack's sweet little voice echoing from his playroom. Each time I am made aware of the many sensory experiences happening around me, I say a silent prayer of gratitude. We spend so much time racing from one activity to the next that we seldom stop to "live" in our bodies. These frequent daily check-ins help me to relax and keep my heart and mind open, which in turn boosts my creativity and benefits every aspect of my life and business.

Taking pause is essential in finding the things that inspire our hobbies and interests. I discovered my love for embroidery when I laid eyes on a quilt an ex-boyfriend had inherited. The stitches were so beautiful and intricate that I studied them carefully and tried to learn how to recreate them. Eventually, this inspired a garment in my clothing line (an item that was worn by Kate Bosworth when she won the date in the movie *Win a Date with Tad Hamilton*).

I found my love of scrapbooking in a similar fashion. I have been a scrapbooker for such a long time that it's easy to forget that I stumbled upon my love for this medium by taking a class at a local store on a whim (see page 90). Although I spent most of my life not engaging with this medium, once I began, it turned out that deep down I had always been a scrapbooker at heart—a natural collector of photos, bits, and little treasures.

What I most love about scrapbooking, and crafting in general, is that every time I fill a page with photographs, quotes, and mementos, I am collecting proof of a good life. I love sifting through the pictures and extracting the moments that mattered most, weaving them all together—memories of love and laughter represented on a single scrapbook layout.

From an outsider's perspective, embroidery and other crafts might seem a little bit Pollyanna-ish. Maybe it is. But for a moment, indulge me, and consider how deep the reflection of modern-day memory-keepers can be. As we look back on our memories, we simultaneously reinforce our core values. The importance of our children, spouses, parents, friends, loved ones, pets, hobbies, and vacations are cemented onto pages with glue and double-sided tape. We remember: *These are the things that make me happy.* We declare who we are as individuals, and we see—in splashes of color, doodles, and journaling—that our lives do not look like anyone else's lives. We get to know ourselves deeply, lovingly, and uniquely.

By its very nature, scrapbooking is a journey into the past. Through documenting, we treasure our triumphs, reflect upon the lessons we have learned, and appreciate the moments of life. What person hasn't looked at the piles of memorabilia waiting to be sorted, only to say, "That went by so fast. How can I ever capture every memory that I want to hold in my heart?" But scrapbooking is also a journey forward. Chronicling our lives can truly inspire us: "What will I do next? How can I give my life more meaning? How can I fill my days with enough excitement and love to justify another scrapbook?"

Looking at our various finished (or even unfinished) craft projects can stir up positive emotions. We are reminded that life is happening. Our passions and hobbies can serve as a reminder to stay present. The creative process of documenting our lives on paper allows us to pause when we take the photos, and then reflect and relive those moments when we scrapbook them. Sharing those memories with loved ones is so special, as is having an archive of those precious moments.

This opportunity for deep reflection is not unique to scrapbooking. Anyone who sits in quiet solitude working on a craft—whether it is knitting a blanket or refurbishing a chair—is simultaneously healing, growing, and contemplating. Alone with our thoughts and our crafts, we cannot help but dive deeply into the recesses of our souls.

So while the world might think crafting is small in the grand scheme of things—that our crafts are hobbies, at best—we know better, don't we?

One of my dreams for this book was that it would serve as both a collection of words, thoughts, and reflections and as an opportunity to heal and grow through the power of crafting. It is a declaration that we all can live our lives uniquely, creatively, and lovingly.

CRAFT A LIFE YOU LOVE

Ruts are often born out of well-intentioned ideas.
Perhaps you stop by the same coffee shop on your way
to work every morning simply because it's on the way,
making it the most convenient option for caffeine.
But what if you allotted yourself an extra half hour
before work and tried a different coffee shop? You never
know... you just might find the best latte you've ever
tasted! Even if it's not life-changing, it *will* add
variety to your routine and start your day off with a
fresh perspective. And sometimes all we need is a fresh
perspective to gain clarity about what we really want
to be doing.

Here are some tips for discovering hobbies that have
been fruitful for me:

1. Take a class in person or online. There are a number
of great online sites that offer free classes, so you
can dabble and not feel like you're investing too much
when it comes to finding what you love.

Take a few minutes to make a list of classes or subjects
that interest you.

_____

_____

_____

_____

_____

_____

_____

2. Travel to a foreign place. I have found that being exposed to different cultures can be inspiring in so many ways. If it's difficult for you to travel outside the country, try traveling outside of your neighborhood. Observe what's going on around you: take in the sights, talk to the locals, and visit local markets to see what artisans are creating.

Where would you travel if you could go anywhere? Include your hometown and jot down local places you have always wanted to explore. Playing tourist in your own city can be so fun!

_____

_____

_____

_____

3. Visit a museum. Remember in school when you were asked to take a sketchbook and draw something you saw while on a field trip? Make up your own rules and spend the afternoon taking things in.

Sketch your ideal museum field trip—make rules that take you outside the box, like an afternoon seeking only art that includes your favorite color or techniques. Even look around your city and have someone take a photo of you in front of a colorful wall or a mural.

_____

_____

_____

_____

_____

4. Ask a friend. Take a cue from what your friends are into—there's a good chance you'll be interested in it as well. Likewise, if you're obsessed with an activity, offer to share it with your friends. In teaching someone else a hobby, you may discover different facets of that hobby that you love as well.

Organize an evening with friends to swap hobbies, or to get together and try a completely new activity. Crafternoons are the best!

_____

_____

_____

5. Try something you never thought you would do. A friend of mine wanted to go skydiving for his birthday and I jumped at the chance to join him. While that has not become a hobby I often partake in (only twice in my life, in fact), it gave me the confidence to believe in myself when trying things out of my comfort zone.

Challenge yourself by making a list of things you never thought that you would do. They don't have to be daredevil pursuits like skydiving. What about speaking—or even singing—in public? What do you daydream of having the courage to do?

_____

_____

_____

_____

I hope you feel inspired to keep those creative juices flowing!

WHAT'S NEXT?

———

The first time that I really felt as if I had made it in my career in the fashion industry was when Fred Segal ordered twenty of my hand-embroidered tank tops. Fred Segal is a retail store on Melrose Avenue in Los Angeles that carries high-end clothes. It is known for discovering designers and setting trends. It's safe to say that landing a line in Fred Segal is a fashion designer's dream.

Fred Segal bought my white, ribbed, hand-embroidered tank tops at $50 apiece and sold them for $110. I was living in Atlanta, but because my mom was working for an airline in Chicago at the time, we were able to immediately book tickets to Los Angeles so that we could go see the tank tops sitting on the racks at Fred Segal. (I told you that my mom is amazing!)

My mom, my cousin, and I landed at Los Angeles International Airport shortly after noon about a week after Fred Segal had received the order. By the time we got the rental car and drove through what I now know as typical Los Angeles traffic, it was 3:00 P.M.

We arrived at the store, and I stared in disbelief at the stack of my tank tops on the shelf. Of twenty, only three were left.

"Excuse me," I asked the sales associate. "Are there more of these tank tops in the back or did you send them to the Santa Monica store?"

"No," she replied, "we just got them in this week, and they have been selling really fast."

A huge smile broke across my face, and I decided to introduce myself. "Oh! I'm actually the designer, Amy Tangerine," I said nervously.

"Nice to meet you," she said. "You should ask the buyer if he wants to order more."

I called him immediately and asked if he wanted to reorder more tank tops.

"No," he replied quickly. I was a little disappointed, but then he followed his curt response with, "What are you going to make next?"

I didn't have an answer at that moment, but I felt excitement knowing that he wanted to see what else we were going to offer.

What's next?

This is a question that drives the fashion industry. Change is constant. Trends come into style and go out of style seasonally. The colors that are trendy today may not be on trend tomorrow. Just when we thought we had put "mom jeans" to bed, high-rise pants come back into style. As a designer, I had to keep on top of the trends. If I wasn't a part of setting them (or at least anticipating them), someone else was going to beat me to it.

The same is true of life. If you don't decide what your life is going to look like in the coming days, it will happen by default. Time will pass, situations will change, and life will move on. You can either be intentional and participate in your life actively, or you can sit back and wait for life to unfold.

I read that the happiest man in the world believed that in order to be truly happy, people must know their three deepest desires, and they must pursue them relentlessly. They are hard to narrow down, but I think mine are: fulfillment, freedom, and fun.

How about you?

What do you want to invite into your life next? Remember, even if you are content and happy now, things might change. So craft a life that you love. Keep in mind that something is going to happen next.

What do *you* want it to be?

Whatever it is, be sure it makes you happy.

CRAFT A LIFE YOU LOVE

What's next for you?

_____

_____

_____

_____

_____

_____

_____

_____

_____

_____

_____

_____

_____

_____

_____

_____

_____

_____

_____

_____

ACKNOWLEDGMENTS

———

To all the creatives who continue to put yourselves out there by sharing your talents and gifts with the world, you are an inspiration. To all the scrapbookers and paper crafters who have used my products alongside personal memories and family albums, thank you. Seeing what you create is by far one of the best parts of my job.

A very special thank you to my mentors who have guided me (probably without even knowing it): Isabel Gonzalez-Whitaker, Marcia Rothschild, Sherry Farrugia, Randa Allen, and Big Mama.

I am so incredibly grateful to my team at American Crafts, Kin Community, and INKED.

Huge thank you to my literary agent, Kate McKean, and everyone at Abrams.

I feel lucky to have some of the best friends in the world, especially Courtney Spanjers Dewey, Courtney Jaye, Kelly McDermott, Dana Colwell, Kara Barefoot, Kristin Harmel, Gillian Zucker, KC Hoos, Joe Simonds, Doug Heslep, Joey Spanjers, Jamie and Chris Waters, Ann-Marie Espinoza, Dana Grueber, Emily Falconbridge, Debika Bhattacharya, Johanna Black, April and Greg Foster, Paige Evans, Kristina Nicolai-White, Allison Kreft, Shanna Noel, Stephanie Carter, Debby Weiss, Nicole Stevenson, Kelly Purkey, Jennifer McGuire, Cathy Vongnaraj, Lauren Hom, Michelle Clement, Ashley Mary, Pam Garrison, Mye De Leon, Elise Blaha Cripe, Jeanne Pritzker, Stephanie Pitts, Lauren Toyota, Lauren Sheffield, Stephanie Ives, Michael Wray, Mi Young, Anita Finkelstein, Mike Kovac, Keeley Whitford, Jill Orobello, Shannon McQuarrie, Stacy Julian, Eri Suzuki, Stephanie Howell, Thomas and Abby Isaf, Daniel Simonds, Katrine Kanner, Allison Newmark, April Berg, Heidi Swapp, Tim Holtz, Ali Edwards, Kayla Aimee, Kim Lieb, Tia Egidi-Clarida, Brian Griffin, Reuben Poswell, Catherine Tachdjian, Megan Hoeppner, Curtis Estes, Jocelyn Baker, Heidi Yuen, Pamelyn Rocco,

Alisha Johns, Erin Ziering, Tori Spelling, the Grotnes family, the Crummies, the Spanjers family, the Duttas, the Singhas, the Voigts, and the Colwells. (I know I am leaving people out. Forgive me, but I had only two pages!)

I am also deeply indebted to all the people who have worn my T-shirts and taken my workshops in person and online. Your smiles and comments inspire me daily. A very special shout-out to those who also have the self-published first edition of this book. Without your support, this dream would not have happened. Fangerines are the best.

A huge thank you to my family. Papa and Mommy, you have always believed in me and my life would not have been this blessed without your continued love and guidance. Thank you both for instilling the values of hard work and happiness. To my grandparents, who are watching over us, I hope that you are proud. Thank you to all my uncles, aunts, and cousins, especially Cindy Liang, Kristi Tan, Sydney Tan, Brian Liang, and Sachi Ramachandran. To Julia, thanks for making Papa so happy. To Ricky, thanks for making Mommy so happy. Thanks to the entire Cangilla family, including Chris, John, Jenny, Rick, Christopher, Joe, Kristin, and, of course, baby Jacob! Our last names may not be the same, but as luck would have it, we are family.

Thank you again to my favorite guys, JC and Jack. You mean the world to me.

ABOUT THE AUTHOR

Amy Tan has always had a creative outlook on life. Growing up in Chicago, she wallpapered her room with pages from fashion magazines and dreamed of a life of visual creativity. By the time she was twenty-three, she had founded the popular and award-winning handcrafted T-shirt line Amy Tangerine, which was featured in hundreds of retail outlets around the world, including Bloomingdale's, Neiman Marcus, and Barneys in New York and Japan.

It wasn't until 2007 that Amy discovered her true passion: scrapbooking. What started as a slice-of-life hobby blossomed into a full-time, fulfilling business venture that includes signature collections with American Crafts, celebrity events, consulting services, and workshops all over the world. Amy has weekly videos on her YouTube channel (youtube.com/amytangerine), where she gets to participate in her favorite crafting activity of all—helping others tap into their creative sides.

When she's not at home in Los Angeles with two mischievous Jack Russell terriers, her longtime partner, JC, and their adorable son, Jack, Amy is traveling, finding great places to eat, and doing her best to enjoy every moment.

She can be reached at:
amytangerine.com
facebook.com/amytangerine
instagram.com/amytangerine
twitter.com/amytangerine
youtube.com/amytangerine
pinterest.com/amytangerine
instagram.com/craftalifeyoulove

Trust the JOURNEY you are on. ▷▷▷▷▷▷▷▷▷▷ KEEP GOING .